Ft. Horváth Benedeknek igaz szeretettel

Endrey Antal

SONS OF NIMROD
The Origin of Hungarians

By the same author
The Future of Hungary

Sons of Nimrod
The Origin of Hungarians

BY

ANTHONY ENDREY

MELBOURNE
THE HAWTHORN PRESS

First Published 1975
© Anthony Endrey
ISBN 0 7256 0130 2

Endrey, Anthony, 1922—
   Sons of Nimrod: the origin of Hungarians— by
Anthony Endrey. — Melbourne: The Hawthorn
Press, 1975.

ISBN 0 7256 0130 2.

1. Hungarians. I. Title.

572.894511

Wholly set up and printed in Australia by
The Hawthorn Press Pty Ltd
601 Little Bourke Street Melbourne 3000

TO MY WIFE JADWIGA

Contents

Illustrations

Acknowledgments

First of all, my thanks go to Professor G. M. Dening of the Department of History, University of Melbourne, for encouraging me to undertake this project and Mr William Culican of the same Department for his supervision and many helpful suggestions. I am also indebted to Dr Alexander Gallus of the Hungarian Institute, Melbourne, for his guidance on various aspects of Hungarian prehistory and his readiness to discuss my ideas as my work progressed. I must also thank the ever-helpful staff of the Baillieu Library, particularly Miss Elizabeth Garran and Mr Patrick Singleton, who obtained much rare research material for me from Europe and America. I was also helped by various members of the Hungarian community in Australia who supplied me with valuable books and articles on the subject, which would not otherwise have come to my notice. My son, Anthony, assisted me with much Biblical learning and references. Last but not least, I thank my wife for her patience and moral support without which this book would not have been written. I have great pleasure in dedicating this book to her.

Foreword

There are few peoples the origin of which has been the subject of so many fanciful theories and so much idle speculation as the Hungarians. Perhaps because they have no known relatives, or not very close ones, at any rate, and are a strange race in the heart of Europe, the Magyars have at times excited hostile feelings among the surrounding nations and this hostility has often clouded the judgment of historians and ethnic theorists dealing with their origins and early history. Indeed, this proud and talented race had a 'hostile press' from the moment of its appearance on the fringes of the West, probably due to its military superiority, and the prejudices implanted in western minds by the contemporary news media lingered long in historical literature. It was thus with some glee that western writers of the Age of Enlightenment began to assign some extremely primitive and backward tribes to the ancestry of the Hungarians, in much the same way as their mediaeval predecessors made them descend from devils and ogres.

All this was diametrically opposed to the traditions of the Hungarians but they protested in vain against the strange relations foisted of them, for the 'objectivity' of western writers soon found support in Hungary itself and was firmly embraced by the Hungarian Academy.

It so happened then that Hungarians were officially declared to be a Finno-Ugrian people, related to the remotest and least-developed branch of that group, and their ancestors were identified as hunters and fishermen of a low degree of development, inhabiting the forest regions of Russia until they were conquered and civilised by a more advanced people of Turkic race.

The writer was brought up on this 'official' theory and duly believed it until well into middle age when he started to have doubts and resolved to investigate matters afresh. He approached the subject with an open mind and, being a lawyer by training, took pains in sifting facts from fiction. As he went along, an entirely different vista opened up before his eyes and many isolated pieces of information, neglected before, began to fall into place. As a gigantic jigsaw puzzle, the origin of the Hungarians commenced to take shape. What the writer saw was very different from the 'official view', but entirely in accord with the national tradition of the Magyars.

There are very few *facts* in this book which have not been previously established by others. What the writer has done, was to put them in the proper context and to formulate his own conclusions. It is only in this way that originality is claimed for this work. It is also in this way only that the writer may have erred. The facts themselves which are called in support of the writer's propositions are clearly established and well-documented. All the writer did was to adopt a new approach.

If the conclusions drawn are, then, somewhat surprising, the writer fully accepts the blame. However, he does so unrepentantly. It was time to tear down false myths. It was time to speak what the writer believes is the truth.

And so, here it is.

ANTHONY ENDREY

Hungarian Institute
Melbourne

CHAPTER 1

The National Tradition

When the Hungarians conquered the Carpathian Basin in 896, they had their own system of writing and presumably also had written records.[1] Due to their conversion to Christianity towards the end of the tenth century, however, and the destruction of 'pagan writings', these records have been lost.

There is also evidence from the earliest times of a strong epic literature, transmitted orally by a class of bards known as *regös* who went around reciting the deeds of the ancestors and national heroes of the Hungarians.[2] This literature, too, was treated with suspicion and contempt under the early Christian era in Hungary[3] and was not written down. Although many traces of it have survived in Hungarian folklore and, as we shall see presently, in mediaeval literature as well, we are not in possession of any actual texts.

In looking for the earliest Hungarian records relating to the origin and ancestral home of the Hungarians, therefore, we are confined to the Latin chronicles written after the conversion of the Magyars to Christianity. As may be expected, these display much biblical learning and a tendency to tailor facts and events — even legendary ones — so as to agree with a literal reading of the Bible and in particular, the Old Testament.

Fortunately for our line of inquiry, there was a highly popular literary form in the Middle Ages known as the *gesta* which concerned itself with the origins and early history of nations and ecclesiastical institutions. In national history, writers of *gestas* usually followed a strictly defined pattern: they commenced with a description of the ancestral home of the people concerned and then dealt with the origin and pagan era of the people.[4] This was followed by an account of their conversion to Christianity and the history of the first Christian kings.

The writers of these *gestas* were usually chaplains of the royal

1

court, chancellors, bishops or monks belonging to the immediate entourage of the king.[5] Besides reflecting the personal cults and traditions of the royal house they served, their writings were also influenced by political trends current in their time.

Comparative analyses of surviving mediaeval chronicles and other records, both Hungarian and foreign, have established that the first Hungarian *gesta*, entitled *Gesta Ungarorum*, was written about 1091 during the reign of Saint Ladislas (1077-1095).[6] The text of this *gesta* has been lost, probably due to the Mongol invasion of Hungary in 1241, during which most monasteries and other centres of learning in the country were destroyed. Thanks to the painstaking researches of Hóman[7], however, we can state with certainty that the first *Gesta Ungarorum* contained, at least in a rudimentary form, elements of the Nimrod-legend (as to which see below), a description of *Ungaria Maior*, the ancestral home of the Hungarians, and the notion of the identity of Huns and Magyars.

This *gesta* was followed by at least two early twelfth century chronicles, containing similar material, which have also been lost.[8]

The first extant piece of Hungarian historical literature is the *Gesta Hungarorum* of the chronicler commonly known as Anonymus. He cannot be called by any better name because the title page of his work, which has come down in a single manuscript, is missing[9] and only his initial P. is given on the next page. Although he identifies himself in his preface as 'the erstwhile notary of the most glorious King Béla of Hungary of blessed memory', even this presents some difficulty as Hungary had four kings by that name. Most historians agree, however, that the reference is to Béla III (1172-1196)[10] and that accordingly — the king being already of 'blessed memory' — Anonymus wrote around 1200.

Anonymus, being a former pupil of the University of Paris,[11] professes to write in a scientific manner, scorning 'the lying tales of peasants and the garrulous songs of players'. In his introduction, he declares that he will set out for the benefit of his whole nation the genealogy of the kings of Hungary and their nobles and how they descended from Scythia and how many kingdoms they conquered, and asserts that he will do so truly and simply, in the best traditions of literate Hungarians of whom the country is justly proud.

Anonymus therefore writes with a strong intellectual bias, if not outright snobbery, and is obviously determined to ignore the oral traditions current among his people in his time. He thus deprives himself of very valuable source material from the outset and for this reason, we cannot look to him for a full statement of the national tradition concerning the origin of the Hungarians.

After stating his intellectual posture, Anonymus gives a description of Scythia, called *Dentumoger* in the language of its inhabitants, which from his data we can roughly identify with the eastern Ukraine. He then deals with the Scythians and relates that that nation obtained the name Magyar after its first king Magog, son of Japhet. It was from the progeny of King Magog that the powerful King Attila was born and after much time, Ügyek, 'a most noble prince of Scythia', father of Almos 'from whom descend all the kings and princes of Hungary'.

Because Scythia had become too small for the great multitude of its people, seven chieftains called *Hetumoger* (seven Magyars) held council and decided to settle in Pannonia (the mediaeval name for Hungary), which they heard to be the country of King Attila, ancestor of Prince Almos.[12] They then elected Almos their leader and set out from Scythia to the west with a large number of the people. On reaching present-day Hungary, Almos relinquished his leadership and his son Arpád was elected in his place.

Anonymus then gives a detailed account of the Hungarian Conquest under the leadership of Arpád which is the main topic of his work. In the course of his story, he repeats a number of times that Almos and Arpád were descendants of Attila, and at one stage he takes Arpád and his leading men to the ruins of Attila's city on the banks of the Danube.[13]

It is clear from the foregoing that Anonymus not only regards Hungarians as Scythians but he also regards all Scythians as Hungarians. Furthermore, he also treats Attila the Hun as a Scythian-Hungarian. Indeed, the word 'Hun' does not occur once in his *Gesta*. His regard for Attila is so high that he persistently

3

calls him king (rex) — and 'a king of great fame and immense power' at that — whereas he only accords Almos and Arpád the title of prince (dux).

Since the king whom Anonymus had served belonged to the House of Arpád, the first Hungarian dynasty which ruled from 896 till 1301, the emphasis placed on the connection with Attila must have been due to the personal traditions of the royal house and it is now generally accepted that the descent of that house from Attila is factual.[14]

Furthermore, the way Anonymus treats Attila and the Scythians in general, makes it clear that in his time, Hungarians already regarded themselves and the Huns as belonging to one nation, and that this belief was fundamental to their national *ethos*. Their identity with the Huns was also the rationale and justification of their conquest of Hungary which they regarded as 'King Attila's country'. In other words, they considered that the country belonged rightfully to them.

On the other hand, the reference to Magog and his father Japhet is pure fabrication, due to the 'scientific' approach adopted by Anonymus and his western learning. Magog and Japhet were in mediaeval times ascribed to the ancestry of all sorts of nations causing trouble in the west, ranging from Huns to Goths,[15] but they were mostly associated with Scythia.[16] This was clearly known to Anonymus and as he also knew that his people originated from that region, he felt duty bound to make them descend from Japhet and Magog.

As already mentioned, Anonymus states that Scythia is called Dentumoger in the language of its inhabitants.[17] In a subsequent passage, however, he appears to suggest that Dentumoger is the name of the Scythian nation itself.[18] At one time, it was considered that this name meant 'Don-mouth Hungary'[19] but it appears more likely that its meaning is 'seven Magyars' in the language of the surrounding Turkic peoples[20] — that is, the same as Hetumoger in contemporary Hungarian — denoting the seven Hungarian tribes which then lived north-east of the Black Sea and later settled in the Carpathian Basin.

Anonymus' zeal in ignoring legends is quite remarkable. He wholly omits the Nimrod-legend, as well as several legends

4

associated with the Hungarian Conquest which are featured in later chronicles and which must have been very popular in his time. This was clearly due, as he takes care to point out himself, to his contempt for the oral tradition handed down by the common people and the bards,[21] but it hardly endeared him to his contemporaries. It is not surprising then that his work exercised no influence whatever on subsequent Hungarian historical literature[22] and was wholly ignored by the Magyars who apparently did not fancy his flagrant disregard for their most sacred national traditions.

The omissions of Anonymus were remedied with a vengeance by Simon Kézai, court chaplain of Ladislas IV (1272-1290). Kézai whose *Gesta Hungarorum*, written around 1282,[23] was the next major Hungarian historical work following Anonymus, was probably encouraged in expounding the most ancient Hungarian legends — which, after all, were of pagan origin — by the fact that his king, also called Ladislas the Cuman after his mother, had a strong oriental and indeed, pagan background.[24] The atmosphere in the royal court was therefore favourable to an open and even defiant declaration of the oriental origin of the Magyars and the restraints which Anonymus, as a former pupil of the University of Paris, may have felt were no longer present.

After indignantly rejecting allegations of Orosius[25] that Hungarians descended from illicit intercourse between devils and Scythian women of loose morals — allegations actually made concerning the Huns and not Hungarians proper — Kézai declares that he is going to set out the true origin and deeds of the Hungarians. What follows then is obviously said with great conviction and must be regarded as a summary of the most ancient traditions of the Hungarians as known in Kézai's time.

Kézai relates that two hundred and one years after the Flood, the giant Menroth, son of Thana of the blood of Japhet, began with the assistance of all his kinsmen to build the tower of Babel. After the confusion of tongues, he moved to the land of Evilath, which is a province of Persia, and there his wife Eneh bore him twin first-born sons, Hunor and Magor. He had many other wives and their descendants form the Persians. These resemble the Hungarians very much and their language differs from Hun-

5

garian in no greater degree than the Thuringian from the Saxon.

When Hunor and Magor came of age, continues Kézai, they moved into a separate tent from their father. One day when they were out hunting, a female deer appeared before them and they gave chase. She led them into the Meotid marshes and then disappeared. After searching for her all over the area and not finding her, they found the country to their liking and as it was suitable for animal husbandry, they sought permission from their father to settle there. Having lived among the Meotid marshes for five years, they went on a rampage with their men and out in the plains they came onto the wives and children of the sons of Belar who happened to be away. They seized them with all their possessions and took them back to Meotis. By chance, two daughters of the Alan king, Dula, were among the children and these were married by Hunor and Magor. All the Huns descended from these captured women. In time, they grew into a mighty nation so that the region could no longer contain them.

Then follows a detailed account of the exodus from Scythia, western conquests and exploits of the Huns, followed by the history of the Magyars. In his story of the Huns — which is now generally known as the Hun Chronicle — Kézai repeatedly refers to them as Hungarians and when he comes to the Hungarian Conquest, he treats it as the return of the same people.

Kézai's *Gesta* proved an immense success. Its contents were adopted by over twenty mediaeval and Renaissance chronicles in Hungary,[26] beginning with the Buda Chronicle (c. 1333)[27] and the Illustrated Chronicle (1358),[28] and right up to the present day Hungarian literature is full of allusions to the Hun connection so clearly declared by him.

Notwithstanding this wholehearted acceptance of Kézai's story by the Magyars, many modern historians have questioned its authenticity and some have gone to the extent of declaring that the whole Hun Chronicle is a thirteenth-century fabrication.[29] The most determined among these is Macartney who in an effort to explain away over twenty early Hungarian sources, the virtually unanimous opinion of western chronicles (see Chapter 2) and the oral traditions of the Hungarian people, still current today, asserts that the Hungarians originally knew nothing of

Attila and his Huns but on hearing themselves being identified
with the Huns by the surrounding Germans, Italians and Slavs,
they eventually adopted 'this interesting, if spurious pedigree'.[30]

This hypothesis, which is entirely unsupported by factual evidence, is quite contrary to common sense and fundamental
human behaviour. True, the surrounding nations identified the
Hungarians with the Huns almost from the moment of their
appearance in the West. It is also true, however, that they did
so in the most abusive terms of vilification.[31] 'Attila' and 'Hun'
were dirty words in mediaeval Europe and if they had been
wrongly applied to Hungarians, the natural reaction on the part
of the latter — especially after their conversion to Christianity
which put them at odds with their pagan past anyway — would
have been to protest loudly against such unjust accusations.
Nothing of the sort happened: on the contrary, the kinship with
Attila and the Huns was proudly proclaimed.

It is unnecessary, however, for us to rely too strongly on an
argument based on human behaviour in the face of calumny,
for an analysis of the Menroth-legend clearly shows that far
from being an inventor of absurdities, Kézai in fact committed
to writing very ancient national traditions which the Hungarians
had brought with them from the East and which contained
many factual elements.

To begin with Menroth himself, all of Kézai's successors, as
well as modern historians, identify him with the biblical Nimrod.
Judging from the elements of Kézai's story, it is possible, and
indeed probable, that he, too, entertained this notion. Nevertheless, he chose to call his man Menroth. Since Kézai, being a
cleric, must have known the correct spelling of Nimrod's name,
his use of a different — one might say, distorted — version indicates that he was relying on oral tradition which was independent of the Bible.[32]

Furthermore, he emphasises, unwittingly perhaps, the want of
association between his story and the Bible by making his Menroth descend from Japhet. That he obviously does so to comply
with the teaching of the early Fathers of the Church, according
to whom the Huns were descendants of Japhet, is besides the
point. What matters is that the biblical Nimrod was a descendant

7

of Cham, as Kézai clearly would have known, yet he, when faced with an obvious difficulty, opts in favour of the Hun connection and Japhet. Indeed, Márk Kálti, the writer of the Illustrated Chronicle (1358), takes up this point and argues that Hunor and Magor could not possibly have been sons of Nimrod, as this is contrary to the Bible. He therefore declares that they were sons of Magog, thus reverting to the 'scientific' mediaeval view. Notwithstanding Kálti's argument, all subsequent Hungarian chronicles show Nimrod as the father of Hunor and Magor.

This persistent identification of Kézai's Menroth with Nimrod might be explained by the suggestion that Nimrod first got into Hungarian folklore from the Bible and that although his name became distorted in the 'lying tales of peasants', nevertheless the association between him and the Bible remained known among educated Hungarians. However, this is extremely unlikely. Biblical references to Nimrod are very scant and they would hardly have been known to ordinary Hungarians. As to Hungarians learned in the Bible, they would have been aware of the teaching of the Church Fathers regarding the descent of the Huns from Japhet, so that if the matter of selecting a biblical ancestor for their people would have been left to them, they would clearly have picked a 'correct' one from Japhet's progeny. Consequently, there is no reason why either group should have adopted the Chamite Nimrod from the Bible.

We are therefore forced to the conclusion that there was a truly original Hungarian tradition concerning Menroth whom the mediaeval Hungarians, seeing the similarities between him and the biblical Nimrod, identified with the latter. This was all the easier as many contemporary Christian sources spelt Nimrod's name 'Nemroth'. It may be useful now for us to investigate whether there were not some more than superficial grounds for this identification.

The Bible contains only three references to Nimrod which are very brief:

> Cush became the father of Nimrod who was the first potentate on earth. He was a mighty hunter before the

8

Lord, hence the saying, 'Like Nimrod, a mighty hunter be-
fore the Lord'. First to be included in his empire were
Babel, Erech and Accad, all of them in the land of Shinar.
From this country came Ashur, the builder of Nineveh,
Rehoboth-ir, Calah and Resen between Nineveh and Calah;
this is the great city. (The last sentence is also read by
some: 'Out of that land he went into Assyria and built
Nineveh and Rehoboth-ir and Calah. . . .') (Gen. 10, 8-12.)

Cush became the father of Nimrod, the first potentate on
earth. (I Chron. i, 10.)

As for Assyria, should it invade our country,
should it set foot on our soil,
we will raise seven shepherds against it,
eight leaders of men,
they will shepherd Assyria with the sword,
and the land of Nimrod with the sword blade.
(Mic. 5, 4-6.)

It is clear from these references that by the time the Genesis
was written (about 950 B.C.),[33] Nimrod had already become a
remote and legendary figure for the Jews.[34] It is also noteworthy
that the cities with the foundation of which he or his successors
were credited were those the ancient Israelites detested most.[35]
Indeed, the very fact that he is listed as a descndant of Cham
probably indicates that the Hebrews regarded him as their traditional enemy[36] and not that he was ethnically a Hamite or that
his skin was black. By the time of Micah (about 730 B.C.), his
identification with the Assyrian oppressors of the Jews was complete.

The Bible knows nothing of Nimrod being the builder of the
Tower of Babel, although the location of this edifice is put on
'a plain in the land of Shinar' (Gen. 11, 2) which is earlier mentioned as the site of Nimrod's original empire. We may also note
here that the structure is described in terms indicating a
Sumerian *zigurrat* ('for stone they used bricks and for mortar
they used bitumen', Gen. 11, 3).

9

On the other hand, Moslem historians clearly ascribe to Nimrod the building of a great tower which he erected so that he might ascend it and see Abraham's God.[37] In Moslem mythology, Nimrod is regarded as Abraham's traditional enemy and a builder of great structures.[38] His name has also been preserved by other peoples in the Near East.

It is also significant that one of the cities the founding of which the Bible attributes to Nimrod or his progeny, Calah, now bears his name and that ancient Borsippa, sister city of Babylon, which local and Jewish tradition associated with the Tower of Babel,[40] is now called Birs Nimrud. According to Moslem historians, the citadel of this city was also built by Nimrod.[41]

Again, part of the old citadel of Edessa (modern Urfa) in north-western Mesopotamia is locally known as 'the throne of Nimrod'. Nimrod's connections with Edessa are particularly close. A mountain in the vicinity of the city is called Nimrud Dagh (Mount Nimrod). According to early Christian legends in the East, dating back to the fourth century, Edessa itself was built by Nimrod after he had migrated there from Babylonia after the Flood and he ruled in the city.[42]

Nimrod is therefore well-attested throughout the Near East as a mighty ruler, the builder of the Tower of Babel and the traditional enemy of Semites. It is, however, extremely unlikely that these matters were known to Kézai. Mediaeval Hungarians had little contact with Arabs or the Near East, save for a solitary Hungarian crusade in 1217 which only lasted four months. Even assuming that some of the Magyar crusaders were able to converse with the natives, it is highly improbable that they discussed Moslem mythology with them, or even if they did, that they picked up pieces of the Nimrod-legend in such discussions, unless Nimrod was an important figure to them by reason of their own traditions. The same answer may be made to any suggestion that the extra-biblical elements of the Nimrod-legend were brought to Hungary by Mohammedan traders. Such casual contacts could scarcely have resulted in widespread acceptance of a supposedly new myth concerning the origin of an entire nation.

It is therefore reasonable to suppose that Nimrod was adopted by the Hungarians as their mythical ancestor — if indeed, it was a matter of adoption and not of direct descent from a Mesopotamian people subsequently symbolised as Nimrod — at a time when Hungarians were living in the Near East in the immediate neighbourhood of Semitic peoples, in close contact with them and most likely engaged in repeated warfare against them.

Turning now to Nimrod's father, Thana, it is possible that his name is derived from *tanhu*, the title of the Hun emperors according to Chinese sources — compare the Japanese *tenno* (emperor) — or from the Turkic root *tan* or *ten* (Tanri, Tengri = God). In either case, the name indicates divine descent.

As regards Nimrod's wife, Eneh, there is a recent theory that her name is of Sumerian origin, meaning 'high priestess'.[43] The older view is that the name means 'female deer' and has a totemistic connotation.[44] Since the Hungarian word for female deer, *ünö*, is very old and must have been the same in Kézai's time, the very use of the form 'Eneh' indicates — assuming the latter view to be correct — that the Nimrod-legend is of considerable antiquity and goes back far into the pre-conquest period of Hungarian history.

The location of Evilath is somewhat of a mystery[45] but the name appears to be a distorted version of the name of the northern Mesopotamian city Eluhat which appears in Assyrian sources in the thirteenth century B.C. and which modern research has identified with Edessa (Urfa).[46] (This view is strengthened by the fact that some later Hungarian Chronicles spell Evilath as 'Eiulath' which is even closer to Eluhat.) In Kézai's time Edessa was already known by that name and by the local Arabic name Orhay or Urhay, so that his use of the name Evilath may be another indication of the independent origin and antiquity of the Hungarian Nimrod-legend.

The story of the hunter-brothers is, of course, a genuine piece of Ural-Altaic folklore. The brothers are invariably the eponymous ancestors of two closely related peoples which have merged into one.[47] Magor clearly stands for Magyar and is probably a yet earlier form of *moger*. As to Hunor, although some writers have suggested that this name is simply a distorted form of the Turkic name of the Magyars, *onugor*, so that the two

11

brothers really represent the same people under two different names,[48] this does not make sense and is contrary to the scheme of similar legends found among other peoples related to the Hungarians. It is significant that on the drinking horn of Chernigov, which is a tenth century work attributed to Hungarian silversmiths, depicting a magic hunt by two hunters, each hunter has distinct characteristics — one being a long-haired, bearded 'Ugrian', the other a shaven-headed 'Turk' — suggesting different ethnic origins.[49] It is therefore more likely that Hunor in fact represents the Huns and that this part of the legend has preserved the memory of a merger between Huns and Hungarians.

The references to Belar and Dula are now generally accepted as indicating close connections and intermarriage between Hungarians and Bulgars and Alans respectively during the preconquest period.[50]

Even the Persians who speak Hungarian can be explained. It is a well-established fact that a branch of the Hungarian people lived south of the Caucasus between the eight and twelfth centuries (if not earlier), wedged between Armenia and Persia.[51] As late as the middle of the tenth century, the Hungarians in the Carpathian Basin maintained close contact with these Hungarians in the Near East.[52] Since the latter were smaller in number, they were presumably under Persian hegemony, if not direct Persian rule, and by the time when contact with them ceased, the Hungarians in present-day Hungary may well have regarded them as Persians.

Kézai's story, therefore, far from being a thirteenth century concoction, is a veritable guidepost of Hungarian prehistory, bearing many markings pointing in various directions. Let us see now whether those markings are supported by the writings and traditions of other peoples which were in contact with the Hungarians before or shortly after their arrival in their present homeland.

CHAPTER 2

Early Foreign Sources

The first source which deals at some length with the movements of the ancient Hungarians is the Poveshti Yearbook,[1] written in Kiev about 1116 but based on much earlier records. The importance of this Yearbook lies in the fact that the Kievans had first-hand knowledge of the Magyars and were able to observe their movements prior to their settlement in their present homeland.

The Poveshti Yearbook begins with the division of the earth between Noah's sons after the Flood and states that Afet (Japhet) received the southern and western parts, down to the mountains of the Caucasus which are called 'the mountains of the Ugors'. In the following narrative which precedes the actual annals and therefore must have been based on oral tradition antedating written records, there are various references to the exploits of White and Black Ugors on the South Russian steppe. In the nomenclature of the peoples of that region, the designations 'white' and 'black' signified two branches of the same people[2] and as we shall see presently, the writer of Poveshti clearly meant one people and one people only by the name Ugor. The first chronological reference to the Ugors is in 898 when the chronicler states that, having arrived from the east, they camped in the vicinity of Kiev and then crossed the great mountains which thereafter were called 'the mountains of the Ugors'. This is followed by a description of the wars of the Ugors with the Slovenes, Vlachs, Greeks and Moravians and it is clear from the context, confirmed by the slightly incorrect dating (the correct date is generally accepted as 896), that the reference is to the Magyar conquerors and that 'the mountains of the Ugors' in this instance signify the Carpathians.

During the following two centuries, Poveshti makes repeated references to the Hungarians, always calling them Ugors (*Ugor,* pl. *Ugri*), and it is interesting to note that St Stephen, first king of Hungary (997-1038), is referred to as 'Stephen the Ugrian'.

Poveshti ends in 1110 and is immediately followed by the Kiev Yearbook (1111-1199), which again refers to the Hungarians several times and invariably calls them *Ougri*. The slightly different spelling is probably due to Byzantine influence and is of no significance.

In subsequent Ukrainian and Russian Yearbooks, the Hungarians are consistently called *Ugri, Ugori* and *Ougri*[3] right up to 1292, when the name *Vengerski* makes its first appearance in the Ipatius manuscript of the Halych-Volodymir Yearbook. This new name was clearly due to Polish influences and can be disregarded for our purposes.

The early Ukrainian and Russian chronicles therefore firmly reserve the name *Ugor, Ugri* for the Hungarians from the earliest times until their settlement in the Carpathian Basin and thereafter for several centuries during their Christian era, as a specific name not applied to any other people. Apart from the significance of the name itself (the origin of which will be discussed in Chapter 8) and the fact that White and Black Ugors clearly signify northern and southern Hungarians, the most important piece of information recorded by these chroniclers is that before the advent of the Hungarians under Kiev, the mountains of the Caucasus were known as 'the mountains of the Ugors'.

Since this name was later applied to the Carpathians of which the Hungarians lived — as viewed from Kiev — on the far side, we must assume that at the time the mountains of the Caucasus acquired the epithet Ugor, the Hungarians also lived on their far side, i.e., south of the Caucasus in Transcaucasia.[4] Indeed, the Kievans would hardly have called the mountains of the Caucasus by that name unless they had to be crossed in order to reach the original home of the Hungarians.

This, of course, is very much in agreement with Kézai, who makes the ancestors of the Hungarians come out from the region of Persia.

Turning now to Byzantine writings, a fruitful source of information concerning peoples inhabiting the South Russian steppes and the Caucasian regions, we find the first references which can be positively identified with the Magyars in 836-38 when they are reported as allies of the Danube Bulgars against the Byzantine fleet on the Lower Danube.[5] At that stage, they are mentioned under three different names: Huns (*unnoi*), Turks (*turkoi*) and Ugors (*uggroi*). The first two were generic names also applied by the Byzantines to other steppe peoples related to the Hungarians but the last one, Ugor, was, at least in the ninth century, a specific name reserved solely for the Magyars and it remained the name by which they were known in later Byzantine and even modern Greek usage.[6]

The fact that at the time of their emergence with a clear national identity, the Hungarians are called by the same specific name in both Ukrainian and Byzantine writings cannot be mere coincidence.

The Byzantine writers who record the Hungarians around 836 — Leo Grammaticus and Georgius Monachus — do not state where they were living at that time or where they had originated from. Several references to Ugors, however, can be found in earlier Byzantine sources. The first of these is Priscus Phetor who reports that in 463, the Saragurs, Urogs and Onogurs, having been ejected from their ancestral homes by the Sabirs, were looking for a new country, and sent legates to the Byzantine Emperor, seeking his alliance.[7] At that stage, the Saragurs had already attacked the Akatsir Huns in their search for a new homeland and defeated them in numerous battles.[8] These references to Sabirs and Akatsirs enable us to fix the location of the Saragurs, Urogs and Onogurs at the time of their appearance as the area north of the Caucasus and east of the Black Sea. The proposed alliance with Byzantium also suggests that the three peoples in question were at that time being pushed towards the Greek settlements on the eastern shores of the Black Sea.

The fact that Saragurs, Urogs and Onogurs make their appearance together and send a joint legation to Byzantium, indicates close connection between them and this is confirmed by an analysis of their names. Saragur can be analysed as a composite of the Turkic *sar* (white) and Ogur or Ugor, corresponding to the White Ugors of the Poveshti Yearbook. Urog is either a misspelling of Ugor[9] or a more ancient version of that name.[10]

15

Onogur is again a composite of the Turkic *on* (ten) and Ogur or Ugor, indicating a federation of ten tribes under Ugor leadership.[11]

The independent appearance of a people called Ugor, accompanied by two other peoples bearing that name in a composite form, strongly suggests that the Ugors were an ancient race of distinction who gave their name to other peoples associated with them.[12]

Priscus does not state where these three peoples had been dislodged from but from the well-attested settlement of the Sabirs in the northern Caucasus at about the same time,[13] it appears that the Ugors, Onogurs and Saragurs previously lived in that region. Indeed, they must have lived on the southern side of the Caucasus at an earlier stage, for Agathias reports that in 554 the Persians occupied a fortress called Onogur in Colchis, which was then of considerable antiquity. Agathias relates that this locality derived its name from 'the Huns called Onogur' who attacked this place in ancient times but were defeated by the Colchians, who thereafter called the fortress Onogur in memory of the aggressors.[14] This is, of course, a 'Greek explanation' which is entirely unlikely and the probability is that the Onogur people lived in that part of Colchis for an extended period some centuries previously, and that the memory of their earlier settlement there was preserved by the fortress in question.

Half a century after Priscus, in 520, we hear of a king of the 'Huns' living in the vicinity of the Cimmerian Bosporus (the Straits of Kerch) whose name was Gord — formed possibly from Ugor with the addition of the old Hungarian diminutive suffix — d. Gord embraced Christianity and became an ally of the Byzantine Emperor but was killed by his people, who elected his brother Muager in his place.[15] Having regard to the eastern custom of naming rulers after the people subject to them, the names of the two brothers suggest very close connection, if not complete identity, between Ugors and Magyars.

Ugors, Onogurs and Saragurs are again mentioned as separate but related peoples by Zacharias Rhetor in his Chronicle written in Syriac, the relevant part of which dates from about 561.[16] A few years later, in 569, a Byzantine envoy named Zemarchos is

16

reported crossing the territory of the Ugors between the Lower Volga and the Kuban rivers. These were friendly to him and his entourage and warned them of a Persian army lurking in the dense forests around the Kuban.[17] At about the same time, Theophylactes Simocatta refers to a people named Ogor which is 'most powerful in numbers and in military experience' and lives near the river Til which the Turks call 'black'.[18] (The 'black Til' is clearly the southern or lower Volga.) He also describes how two other peoples originated from this people and called themselves Avars on settling in the west.

The name Ugor appears again in a letter written by Joseph, king of the Khazars, early in the tenth century where he lists Ugor as the eldest of the ten 'sons' of Togarma, a descendant of Japhet, giving him precedence over Huns, Avars and his own Khazars.[19]

To complete the picture, it is interesting to note that when the Magyars first emerge in the west by attacking the eastern Frankish Empire in 862, Hinkmar of Rheims refers to them as 'unknown enemies called Ugri'.[20] The Annales Sangallenses Maiores continuously refer to the Hungarians as 'Agarens' from 888 to 955,[21] and although this name is clearly misconceived, signifying Saracen or Arab in the nomenclature of that era, it again brings to mind the name Ugor. The Bavarian historian Aventinus, writing in the Renaissance period, still calls the Hungarians 'Ugri' who in their own language are 'Magyars'.[22]

We therefore find a continuous record of the Ugors from the Caucasian region through the South Russian steppes to present-day Hungary, at the end of which journey they are in the most specific terms identified with the Magyars by Byzantine, Slav and German writers. Since all the sources reviewed by us refer to Ugors as a particular people and not as a group of peoples or steppe-dwellers in general, we are justified in assuming that at all stages of their appearance in history, the Ugors represent the Magyars and no other nation.

Nothing further is heard of the Saragurs after the sixth century but Arab sources based on ninth century records refer to a substantial branch of Magyars settled between the middle Volga and the southern slopes of the Urals, in the vicinity of present-day Bashkiria.[23] These Magyars were separated from the main body of Hungarians and probably moved to the location referred to in the seventh century when a branch of the Bulgars left the Caucasian region and migrated north-eastward to found Magna Bulgaria on the Volga.[24] It is reasonable to suppose that these Magyars formed the northern branch of Hungarians — the White Ugors or Saragurs — even before their final separation, and since their migration so far from the Caucasus put them outside the Byzantine sphere of interest, it is understandable that they do not thereafter appear in Byzantine records. They preserved their ethnic identity, however, for several centuries and still spoke 'pure Hungarian' when the monk Julian found them in 1237.

References to the Onogurs also peter out towards the end of the seventh century. They are last mentioned as an existing people in 671 when Theophanes refers to them as living north of the Black Sea in the region of the Don and the Cimmerian Bosporus, in company with the Bulgars and the Kotragurs.[25] Nearly three centuries later, Constantinus Porphyrogenetus states that the Danube Bulgars were once called Onogurs.[26] Although the Onogurs and the Bulgars were listed as separate peoples as early as the sixth century,[27] it appears from Arab and Persian writings based on an early tenth century Arab source that the name Onogundur or a corrupted form of it, Vanandur or Vunundur, ultimately fastened onto the Danube Bulgars and was regarded as their proper name.[28] This is confirmed by the mediaeval Hungarian name of the Danube Bulgars, *Nándor*.[29] All this suggests that the Onogurs were closely related to the Bulgars and excludes any possibility that the Hungarians descended from them as some historians maintain.

The Turkic etymology of the names of the Onogurs and Saragurs and the fact that the name Ugor forms part of both of these names, however, strongly argue in favour of an extended association between Hungarians and certain Turkic peoples of whom the Onogurs must have been one. In view of the close relationship between and possible identity of Onogurs and Bulgars, it is probably this association with the Onogurs which forms the factual basis of the rape of the daughters of Belar in the Nimrod-legend.[30]

Even apart from this Onogur connection, the Hungarians must have lived in a Turkic milieu for several centuries, intermarrying with and assuming many of the characteristics of Turkic peoples and resulting in their being referred to as 'Turks' and 'Huns' in various Byzantine and Arab writings. This Turkic association is confirmed by the company in which the Hungarians make their appearance from time to time between the fifth and ninth centuries A.D. and as we shall see later, also their predominantly Turkish ethnic character and culture at the time of their settlement in the Carpathian Basin.

This Turkic association finds further support in the chapters relating to the Magyars in Constantinus Porphyrogenetus' *De administrando imperio*, a most important source written around 949.[31] Since Constantinus, a Byzantine Emperor, also throws some light on the earlier homes and origin of the Hungarians, we shall deal with this writing of his in some detail. Constantinus relates that the Magyars whom he calls Turks (*turkoi*), originally lived in a place called Lebedia where they were known as *Sabartoi asphaloi*. After being defeated by the Petchenegs (a Turkic people), they split into two parts. One part went eastward and settled in the region of Persia where 'they to this day are called' by the ancient denomination of the Turks 'Sabartoi asphaloi'. The other part went west and settled in places called *Atelkuzu* (Hungarian *Etelköz*, 'between the rivers', 'Mesopotamia'). After another defeat by the Petchenegs, this western branch settled in present-day Hungary.[32]

Constantinus does not give any dates for these events but we know from the Frankish writer Regino that the Hungarians were living at the mouth of the Don in 889 when they were expelled from there by the Petchenegs. It is accepted by most modern historians that this was the time and place of the first defeat of the Hungarians by the Petchenegs referred to by Constantinus.[33] It would follow from this that Lebedia was near the mouth of the Don, but its precise location is still subject to argument. It may have been identical with the Dentumoger of Anonymus but it also could have been an intermediate home between the latter and Atelkuzu. The name itself is definitely not of Hungarian origin and of the various etymologies which have been given for

19

it, the most likely seems to be that it comes from the Russian *lebed* (swan), meaning swan-country. This would accord with Kézai's report that after leaving Persia, Hunor and Magor lived among the Meotid marshes.

Atelkuzu is better defined by Constantinus, being the region or regions between the Bug, Sereth and Pruth rivers. Judging from the date given by Regino for the eviction of the Magyars from the Don (889) and the date of their settlement in the Carpathian Basin (896), the time spent by them in Atelkuzu must have been comparatively short.

The meaning of *Sabartoi asphaloi* is again hotly contested but most historians agree that whatever the origin of this expression, it refers — insofar as it relates to the Magyars settling in the region of Persia — to the branch of Hungarians reported in Armenian and Arab sources from the eighth century onwards as living near the river Kur in Transcaucasia.[34] The Armenians called this people *Sevordik* and this appears to correspond with *Sabartoi*, whilst *asphaloi* is simply a Greek adjective meaning 'mighty' or 'glorious'. It cannot be correct, of course, that these Hungarians migrated to Transcaucasia after the defeat inflicted on their people in Lebedia by the Petchenegs, since they appear in Armenian and Arab sources as living south of the Caucasus nearly a hundred and fifty years earlier. We must assume, therefore, that the story of the split is either a speculative explanation by Constantinus for the presence of the same people in two places so distant from one another, or it refers to a comparatively small number of Magyars seeking refuge with their kinsmen in Transcaucasia after the defeat of their main body by the Petchenegs.

A number of matters of importance must be noted in connection with these eastern Hungarians. Firstly, the Magyars in present-day Hungary still sent envoys to them 'in the parts of Persia' at the time when Constantinus wrote and exchanged messages with them.[35] There is no record of similar contacts between the western Hungarians and the other branch of Hungarians in the east near Bashkiria to whom we have already referred. Indeed, when the monk Julian found them in 1237, he did so virtually by accident.[36] We must assume, therefore, that the western Hungarians and the Hungarians in Transcaucasia both belonged to the southern branch of the Magyars and remained in close contact over a long period, whilst the Magyars near Bashkiria represented a northern branch which separated from the other two at a much earlier date.

The second matter is that according to Constantinus, the Magyars in Lebedia consisted of seven tribes and he gives their names with what appears to be reasonable accuracy.[37] Now, we know from Anonymus that all seven tribes — the Hetumoger — migrated to the west. Consequently, no substantial part of the Lebedian Hungarians could have remained behind and the Transcaucasian Hungarians could not have originated from them. Nevertheless, Constantinus asserts that both the Lebedian and the Transcaucasian Hungarians were called *Sabartoi asphaloi*. This identity of designation again confirms that these two branches of Hungarians must have formed a closely united people over an extended period.

Thirdly, the Transcaucasian Hungarians were still called *Sabartoi asphaloi* in Constantinus' time, although their western brothers had by then long lost that name. This suggests that the name itself was of Transcaucasian origin and that the Lebedian Hungarians acquired it while they were living in that region.

Lastly, the place where Constantinus puts the Transcaucasian Magyars coincides with the north-western region of the Persian Empire from the fourth century onwards,[38] an area for the possession of which Byzantium and Persia fought a series of fierce wars in the fifth and sixth centuries.[39] This again confirms Kézai's assertion that the Magyars originated in Persia and also supplies a likely explanation for their northward movement.

To summarise, the matters recorded by Constantinus raise the possibility that originally all Hungarians lived south of the Caucasus and that their division, due to a desire to avoid enslavement by the great powers contending for their homeland, occurred in two stages: first by the separation of the White Hungarians later found near Bashkiria, and then by the settlement of the main body of Magyars on the shores of the Black Sea. The Sevordiks south of the Caucasus thus represented those who remained behind in the ancient home of all Hungarians.

21

Probing further in the Transcaucasian region for evidence in support of these suppositions, we find it recorded by Theophylactes Simocatta[40] that in 587, two Byzantine generals restored in Armenia 'the fortress of the Matsars, ruinous with old age'. This fortress must have been erected, therefore, by a people of that name some centuries previously. It is significant that in modern Turkish, the word for Hungarian is still *Macar* (pronounced as Matsar), indicating local survival of this form of Magyar.

Another Byzantine writer, Agathias, when reporting on the war between the Greeks and the Persians in Colchis in 554, refers to a fortified town called Mukheir.[41] Writing about the same campaign, Procopius states that an entire province of Colchis is called Mukheris and that it is thickly populated and by far the best part of the country.[42] These geographical designations clearly bring to mind the name Moger preserved by Anonymus and indicate the presence of a people of that name over an extended period.

The reader will recall that it is in the same year and in the same province that Agathias reports the occupation of a fortress called Onogur by the Persians. Hungarians and Onogurs must have been therefore associated south of the Caucasus centuries before their emergence on the northern side.

Indeed, strong evidence of Hungarian presence in Transcaucasia well before Christ can be found in the writings of Herodotus and Xenophon. Reporting on the wars of Cyrus in the middle of the sixth century B.C., Herodotus refers repeatedly to a people called Makrones living in the neighbourhood of Colchis and Cappadocia and furnishing soldiers for the army of the great Persian king.[43] More details of this people are supplied in Xenophon's Persian Expedition, written at the beginning of the fourth century B.C. Xenophon reports that as the Greek army was crossing the mountains north of Armenia, marching through the country of the Scytheni on its way to the Black Sea, it was held up at a river forming the boundary between the Scytheni and the Makrones. The latter were drawn up in battle order, ready to impede the progress of the Greeks, and it is clear from the narrative that they were sizeable enough to have been able to do so. After the Greeks had pledged their peaceful intentions, however, the Makrones gave them every assistance and led them through their country for three days until they brought them to the Colchian frontier.[44]

The name Scytheni has been interpreted as possibly relating to a party of Scythian invaders.[45] We are justified in suspecting a similar distortion in the name of the Makrones. As the memory of this people has survived in the name of a local mountain called Makur Dagh,[46] it is almost certain that at the time when Herodotus and Xenophon wrote, they called themselves Makor, or a name sounding like that to Greek ears, leading us unerringly to Magor, the eponymous ancestor of the Hungarians and the oldest form of Magyar known to the Hungarians themselves.[47]

The presence of a branch of the Scythians in that area probably gave rise to the first substantial intermarriage between Hungarians and Turkic peoples of which we shall see more later.

To complete our references to the Makrones, it is interesting to note that the second son of Mithridates the Great, Makares, was king of Colchis at the beginning of the first century B.C.[48] Calling to mind the eastern custom of naming the ruler after the people subject to him, the existence of a people called Makar or Magar in that region is clearly postulated.

Before leaving the eastern sources relating to the early Magyars, we must note another important piece of information revealed by Constantinus Porphyrogenetus in his *De administrando imperio*. Constantinus tells us that in leaving Lebedia, the Hungarians were joined by three tribes of the Kabars, a Turkish people. Later on he mentions that the Magyars of his time were, in addition to their own language, also speaking the language of the Kabars. The Hungarians of the Conquest period were therefore bilingual, speaking their present-day language and also a Turkish idiom, and this bilingualism continued up to the middle of the tenth century (when Constantinus wrote) and presumably for some time thereafter. This fact, when looked at in conjunction with other Turkish characteristics of the early Hungarians, suggest a merger between two peoples which is very much in line with the Nimrod-legend and will be further examined in Chapters 4 and 5.

We have left the Western sources last, as by necessity, they only contain first-hand information regarding the Hungarians from the second half of the ninth century. Some of this information, however, is highly significant.

The first important matter emerging from these sources is that from the moment of the appearance of the Magyars in the West in 862 until well into Renaissance times, virtually all Western writers assume their identity with the Huns.[49] This is of course in full agreement with the Hungarian national tradition set out in Chapter 1 and the only logical explanation is that the Western sources derived this notion from the Hungarians themselves. The historical and ethnic bases of this Hun-Magyar identity will be discussed in Chapters 4 and 5.

Another significant piece of information is handed down by two thirteenth-century encyclopaedists, Bartholomaeus Anglicus (fl. c. 1220-1240) and Vincent de Beauvais (c. 1190-c. 1264), who report independently of one another yet in virtually identical terms that the original home of the Hungarians was in outer Syria (*ulterior Syria*).[50] This suggestion is not as absurd as it may seem at first sight. Herodotus tells us that the ancient Greeks called the Cappadocians Syrians[51] and it is almost certain that both Bartholomaeus Anglicus and Vincent de Beauvais refer to Cappadocia. The almost verbatim agreement of the relevant passages of these two authors suggests that they were using a common text since lost, and the reference by both of them to Orosius indicates the original author of that text. Orosius, however, wrote around 415 and could scarcely have referred to the Hungarians. It is more likely that he wrote about the Huns and that some subsequent writer or writers applied his information to the Hungarians. Assuming this to have been the case, we have here a strong mediaeval tradition, dating back to the early part of the fifth century, that contrary to all present-day notions, the original home of the Huns was in Transcaucasia. The ready identification of the Magyars with the Huns in that locality also suggests the existence of a further mediaeval tradition, probably handed down by a series of lost sources, that the Hungarians themselves originally lived in the region of Cappadocia. Since both Bartholomaeus Anglicus and Vincent de Beauvais were highly learned men, the existence of such a tradition seems much more likely than that they uncritically accepted the substitution of Hungarians for Huns in some earlier source.

This suggestion is confirmed by the strong and detailed argument of the Polish historian and geographer Matthias Miechovius concerning the ancestral home of the Huns and Magyars. In his *Tractatus de duabus Sarmatiis,* written at the beginning of the sixteenth century, he devotes a long chapter to the 'Ihuri' (by which name he calls both Huns and Hungarians) and states that these were later called 'Hugui' and then Hungarians. He places the original home of this people in Sarmatia which he describes as the country bounded by the Caspian Sea, the Black Sea and the mountains of the Caucasus. He then takes issue with 'certain historians' who assert that the 'Hugui' came from a land among high and inaccessible mountains. Although he does not specify these mountains by name, it is reasonably clear from his context that he is referring to the Caucasus. There must have been, therefore, a well-established historical tradition even in Renaissance times that the Hungarians originated from Transcaucasia, the strength of which is underlined by Miechovius' efforts to refute it.

Lastly, beginning with Godfried of Viterbo's *Memoria Seculorum* (1185), several Western sources state that the old home of the Hungarians was near the Meotid marshes. This is again in agreement with Kézai and other early Hungarian writers and, as already suggested, may well correspond with Constantinus' Lebedia.

We may now summarise the information imparted to us by foreign sources relating to the Hungarians. They lived originally south of the Caucasus, in the region between Cappadocia and Colchis. Whilst there, they mixed with certain Turkic peoples. In company with these peoples, they moved north of the Caucasus in the early part of the fifth century A.D. They then remained between the Black Sea and the Caspian Sea for four centuries (apart from their northern branch which settled near Bashkiria in the seventh century), until they moved to the Don in the ninth century. After suffering a defeat by the Petchenegs in 889, they shifted to the Western Ukraine, and in 896 they embarked on the conquest of the Carpathian Basin. At some stage during their wanderings, they became so closely identified with the Huns that on their arrival in their present-day homeland, all the surrounding nations regarded them as Huns, as indeed they did themselves.

It is interesting to see how badly this information has fared at the hands of later historians and ethnic theorists.

CHAPTER 3

Fish-Smelling Relations

When the great Hungarian lawyer, Stephen Werböczi, codified
the laws of Hungary in 1514, he was still able to assert as the
fundamental and incontrovertible argument for the original
equality of all Hungarians that 'they all descended from one
and the same stock, namely, from Hunor and Magor.'[1]

This conviction in the absolute truth of the brotherhood of
Huns and Hungarians and their descent from Scythia, remained
basic to the Hungarian ethos for the next two centuries. Even the
Near Eastern origin of the two eponymous ancestors remained
unchallenged and was even embellished by Hungarian historians
of a theological orientation who went to much trouble to find
Persian and Hebrew ancestors for their people through analysis
of the old Testament and comparative linguistics of a rudimentary kind.[2] These efforts to connect Huns and Hungarians
with biblical times lasted well into the eighteenth century and
underwent an enthusiastic revival and extension in the first half
of the nineteenth century when the popular, although uncritical,
professor of history at the University of Budapest, István Horváth, indiscriminately linked the ancestors of the Magyars with
almost every ancient civilisation then known.[3]

The first blow to the national pride was dealt by János Sajnovics, a Hungarian Jesuit, who went to observe the transit of
Venus from the island of Vardö in Norway and on finding similarities between his native tongue and the language of the Lapps
in the vicinity, published a learned thesis in Copenhagen in
1770 (*Demonstratio Idioma Ungarorum et Lapponum idem
esse*), asserting that the language of the Hungarians and the
Lapps was the same.

Five years later, George Pray, 'the father of Hungarian historiography', published his *Dissertationes Historico-Criticae in
Annales Veteres Hunnorum, Avarum et Hungarorum* (Vienna,

27

1775) in which he adopted the findings of Sajnovics, and enlarging these with detailed comparisons between Hungarian and various Finno-Ugrian languages and referring copiously to foreign writers, asserting the relationship between Hungarians and the latter, declared that the Finns and their near relatives were of Hunnish stock and of the same origin with Huns, Avars and Hungarians. He even made an attempt to trace the migrations of these peoples from Karelia, correcting the views expressed by him in an earlier work where he placed the ancestral home of the Huns in Mongolia, north of China.[4]

Whilst the endeavour to classify the Finns as Huns is illuminating because it shows the depth to which the notion of Hun-Magyar brotherhood had permeated the Hungarian mind, it did nothing at the time to allay the consternation of Hungarians who were not at all amused and protested loudly against the 'fish-smelling relations'.[5] The national memory of the Magyars had preserved no trace of any contact with Finns and related peoples and Hungarian public opinion found the way of life of these poor relations as foreign as their political condition uninspiring.

However, the die had been cast. Due to the influence of Pray and a succession of zealots committed to the cause of Finnish-Hungarian relationship, the study of Hungarian prehistory soon became dominated by the Finno-Ugrian school which based its arguments almost entirely on linguistic considerations. This linguistic approach was obvious in the writings of the first major foreign protagonist of this school, August von Schlözer, and his Hungarian disciple, Samuel Gyarmathy, who published a thesis on this subject in 1799. In another age, attempts to explore Hungarian prehistory solely by means of comparative linguistics probably would not have aroused more than a mild and somewhat sceptical interest. The end of the eighteenth and the beginning of the nineteenth centuries, however, witnessed an enormous revival of Hungarian literature and the sudden focussing of public attention on the Hungarian language, previously neglected due to the official use of Latin, lent a reflected glory to the comparative study of that language and supplied the sails of the Finno-Ugrian school with much-wanted wind.

So it happened that when the Hungarian Academy of Sciences

came into existence in 1840, one of its first tasks was to grant generous financial support to a young Hungarian, Antal Reguly, aged only twenty-one at the time, to enable him to establish the relationship between Hungarian and the Finno-Ugrian languages.[6] Reguly made extensive journeys in Karelia and Lappland and finally ended up studying the languages of two small peoples in Western Siberia, the Voguls and the Ostyaks, who were hardly known at that time. He returned to Hungary in 1848, bringing with him a mass of material which, due to his declining health and his early death in 1858, he was unable to publish.[7]

Reguly's inheritance was embraced with great zeal by Paul Hunfalvy whose influence on the study of Hungarian prehistory can be felt even today. In a lecture delivered at the Hungarian Academy of Sciences in 1851, Hunfalvy proclaimed it to be the sacred duty of Hungarians to assume leadership in the field of Finno-Ugrian linguistics and having secured financial support from the Academy, he founded the periodical *Magyar Nyelvészet* (Hungarian linguistics) in 1856, devoted principally to this cause.[8] Hunfalvy was a man of strong convictions who knew no limits in defending his point of view and attacked with great fervour all linguists holding different ideas concerning the origin and relatives of the Hungarian language. He managed to bring the linguistic section of the Hungarian Academy entirely under his sway and when the Academy founded its own linguistic periodical, the *Nyelvtudományi Közlemények*, in 1861, Hunfalvy was appointed its editor and remained in this position for the next fourteen years. During this period, he published a Lapp grammar and two substantial treatises on the Vogul and Ostyak languages.

Hunfalvy found an able and learned collaborator in Joseph Budenz, a young philologist from Göttingen, who specialised originally in Indo-European languages but became soon attracted by the virtually unknown territory of Ural-Altaic languages[9] and was invited by Hunfalvy to settle in Hungary. From the late 1850's, Budenz was the most frequent contributor to Hunfalvy's periodical and, next to him, the chief protagonist of the Finno-Ugrian school. He was the first trained linguist to enter the field of Finno-Ugrian comparative philology — Hunfalvy himself was

29

a dilettante — and applied the methods of Indo-European linguistics to his new-found field of interest. Whether these methods were entirely suited to the subject matter is another question.

In 1864, Hunfalvy published a voluminous work entitled *A vogul föld és nép* (*The Vogul country and people*), based on Reguly's researches. Budenz showed more originality and as a result of his own efforts, compiled a Hungarian-Finno-Ugrian comparative dictionary (1873-81) and also published a comparative morphology of the Finno-Ugrian languages (1884-94).

Due to the joint and tireless efforts of Hunfalvy and Budenz, the Finno-Ugrian origin of the Hungarian language became generally accepted in scientific circles. However, whilst Budenz contented himself with linguistic studies, Hunfalvy transferred his linguistic conclusions to the field of prehistory and declared that the Magyars were of Finno-Ugrian ethnic origin.[10]

This entirely unwarranted transposition of linguistics into ethnic theory has ever since dominated the study of Hungarian prehistory, not only in Hungary but also abroad. Indications furnished by linguistic research, sparse as they were, were magnified out of all proportions and the proud inheritors of Attila's sword were boldly pronounced as basically of humble Finno-Ugrian stock. Indeed, 'denounced' would be the more appropriate expression, for certain foreign scholars, mainly Germans — such as Zeuss, Büdinger and Roessler — hardly concealed their hate towards the Hungarians and their pleasure in tearing down the 'myths' of this troublesome race,[11] whilst their confreres in Hungary followed the same path out of a desire to keep up with, and if possible, outdo, the western Joneses. It is not surprising then that scientific objectivity was often lost in this fervour to create a Finno-Ugrian prehistory for the Hungarians.

Because studies of Finnish and languages more closely related to it did not produce sufficiently strong indications of ethnic relationship with the Magyars, attention was increasingly focussed on the Voguls and Ostyaks, also called Ob-Ugrians by reason of their settlements along the river Ob in Western Siberia. Bernát Munkácsi, Károly Pápai and Joseph Pápay, all Hungarians, carried out particularly intensive researches among these peoples towards the end of the nineteenth and the beginning of

the twentieth centuries, whilst among foreign scholars, A. Ahl-
quist and S. Patkanov distinguished themselves in the same
field.[12] Although these studies indicated a closer relationship of
Hungarian with Vogul and Ostyak than with the other Finno-
Ugrian languages, the conclusions drawn from them by certain
historians and ethnic theorists were entirely unjustified.

A great deal of the blame attaches to Budenz' foremost disciple, Joseph Szinnyei who, after distinguishing himself in Finno-
Ugrian linguistics,[13] turned to Hungarian prehistory and basing
his assertions entirely on linguistic researches, attributed to the
ancient Magyars an exclusively Finno-Ugrian origin and civilisation.[14] His 'crowning achievement' was the publication of a
voluminous manual of Hungarian linguistics (*Magyar Nyelvtudomány Kézikönyve*) by the Hungarian Academy of Sciences in
1923 which devoted a separate volume to Hungarian prehistory,
based largely on an analysis of the basic vocabulary of Hungarian. The writer of this volume, Istvan Zichy,[15] undoubtedly
influenced by Szinnyei, concluded that the social organisation
and civilisation of the ancient Magyars corresponded with those
of the present-day Ob-Ugrians and that the original home of the
Hungarians was in the forest region of the Urals, near where the
Voguls were still living in the eighteenth century.[16] This kind of
idle speculation proved too much even for foreign scholars.
Sauvageot[17] and Tallgren[18] were quick to point out that the
Voguls and Ostyaks were exhibiting signs of regression and
probably had a higher degree of civilisation previously, whilst
Wiklund expressed the view that these two peoples were ethnic-
ally not Finno-Ugrians and had acquired their present language
through outside contacts.[19]

At the time these discussions were taking place, there was
already a substantial literature dealing with certain basic words
of Turkic origin in Hungarian and their importance as regards
the ethnic origin of the Hungarian people. Under the influence
of linguists, however, these Turkic elements in the Hungarian
language were regarded as 'loan-words' of little significance,
indicating no more than neighbourly contacts with, and at most,
conquest and domination by, a Turkic people or peoples.[20]

Although the following fifty years saw more research into and

31

discussion of the Turkic aspects of Hungarian, the basic assumption of the Finno-Ugrian ethnic origin of the Magyars has not been successfully challenged. Linguists have continued to transpose their findings directly into ethnic theory[21] and the eminent Hungarian prehistorian, Gyula László, whilst occasionally bemoaning the domination of linguistics in the study of Hungarian prehistory,[22] has only recently reaffirmed that 'the Hungarian language and through it, our Finno-Ugrian relationship, are, as before, safe bases of our researches into prehistory'.[23]

We may now state briefly the Finno-Ugrian ethnic theory in its present-day form. According to this theory, the ancestors of the Finno-Ugrian peoples lived on the European side of the Urals around the rivers Kama and Pechora in the forest zone at the beginning of the third millenium B.C. They formed a homogeneous group until about 2500-2000 B.C. when the Finno-Permic group moved towards the west and north-west and the Ugric group migrated gradually towards the south-east. However, this was a slow process and the various groups remained in contact over a considerable period. The separation of the proto-Hungarians from the Ob-Ugrians took place about 500 B.C. The Hungarian ethnic group moved towards the borders of the forest zone and settled at the outer tracts of the steppe, in the region of present-day Bashkiria. There they made contact with Turkic tribes presumably of Turco-Bulgar origin and under their influence, adopted a semi-nomadic, horsebreeding way of life. During the thousand years following their separation from the Ob-Ugrians, certain amalgamation took place between the proto-Hungarians and Turkic elements, so that at around the fifth century, A.D., we find a Hungarian people exhibiting mainly Turkic features and living in a Turkic environment. At that time, the Finno-Ugrian peoples, including the Hungarians, were still living in the area demarcated in the east by the Urals, in the north by the Arctic Sea, in the east by the Gulf of Bothnia and the Baltic Sea and in the south by the line Libau-Novgorod-Tambov-Saratov-Jekaterinburg. The Hungarians who were living in the south-eastern region of this area, were then swept south and westwards by the great migration of peoples, until they eventually landed in present-day Hungary.[24]

Apart from the fact that most members of the Finnish group still live within the area stated, that the Ob-Ugrians were living there around 1300 A.D. and that a branch of Hungarians was found in the vicinity of Bashkiria by the monk Julian in 1237, the entire Finno-Ugrian theory is *purely speculative* and both the stages and the timetable of the suggested separation are based entirely on comparative linguistics.[25] In particular, apart from the existence of the northern Hungarians referred to, there is no evidence whatever to suggest the presence of the Hungarians within the area stated at any historical or indeed, pre-historic period and their supposed cohabitation with other Finno-Ugrian peoples is just as fanciful as the development attributed to them under Turkic influence between 500 B.C. and 500 A.D.

It is clear therefore, that in order to maintain credibility, the Finno-Ugrian theory must rely heavily on three factors:

(1) The Hungarian language and its progressive relationship with other Finno-Ugrian languages;

(2) The alleged close ethnic relationship between Hungarians and the Ob-Ugrians; and

(3) The supposition that the branch of Hungarians found near Bashkiria represented those Hungarians who had remained behind in their ancestral home.

As regards linguistic affinity, the number of Hungarian words to which a Finno-Ugrian origin has been attributed, is somewhat less than a thousand.[26] This is in itself a very insignificant number in a language boasting some 190,000 primary words,[27] although the words in question are of a basic character (some personal pronouns, simple numerals, parts of the body, words designating kinship, simple objects, general phenomena of nature, certain plants, animals, parts of the house, simple tools, weapons, items of clothing and verbs denoting everyday actions).[28] It must be pointed out at once that the majority of these words of allegedly Finno-Ugrian origin can only be related to Vogul and Ostyak and have no parallels in the other Finno-Ugrian languages. However, even this number of less than a thousand is grossly inflated. As Dennis Sinor, a Hungarian linguist living in the United States, pointed out in recent years in a trenchant criticism of the past methods of Hungarian linguists, far too many etymologies claiming a Finno-Ugrian connection for certain words had been based on an *a priori* historical hypothesis that these words must be of Finno-Ugrian origin because Hungarians were of such ethnic origin themselves.[29] Indeed, Vámbéry demonstrated nearly a century ago[30] that a number of Hungarian words claimed to have a Finno-Ugrian derivation can be better explained from Turkic languages and a similar study has recently been carried out by Sándor Csöke.[31] It is significant that the Fenno-Ugric vocabulary of Collinder[32] only lists some four hundred and fifty Hungarian words as of Finno-Ugrian origin.[33] If we remove the Ob-Ugrians from the picture, the number of these words falls well below two hundred.

By way of contrast, Hungarian contains at least three hundred words of Bulgaro-Turkic origin, most of which are just as basic in character as the much-stressed Finno-Ugrian vocabulary.[34] If words erroneously listed as Finno-Ugrian are re-classified as Turkic, this number can be probably doubled. Furthermore, it is now reasonably clear that there are at least several hundred, and probably much more, basic words in Hungarian which have Sumerian etymologies.[35]

The Finno-Ugrian words in Hungarian are therefore in the minority even among words of the most basic character and whilst they indicate a certain connection between Hungarian and the Finno-Ugrian languages, such connection is of a very remote nature.

Comparisons of grammatical structures produce no better results. Hungarian is, of course, an agglutinative language and in this it shares common features with all the Ural-Altaic languages and also with many others, such as Japanese and Sumerian. However, when it comes to comparison of specific grammatical phenomena, and in particular, endings and suffixes, Hungarian has very little in common with the Finno-Ugrian languages and, indeed, there are several instances where it is closer to Turkic.[36] Here again, such similarities as exist with Finno-Ugrian languages are to be found mainly in Vogul and Ostyak.

The phonetic relationships of Hungarian and the Finno-Ugrian languages also display similar differences and in certain respects, the phonetics of Hungarian are closer to Turkic languages.[37]

Indeed, Géza Bárczi, the eminent Hungarian linguist, makes the following interesting admission:

> The relationship existing between the Finno-Ugrian languages in their present form is not striking at first sight. It certainly does not even approach the resemblances of diverse members of the Romance or Germanic group . . . but might best be compared to the kinship existing between the different groups of the Indo-European family, e.g. the Germanic and the Slav group.[38]

In other words, each member of the Finno-Ugrian branch of languages may be considered as forming a separate group of its own. Since the Finno-Ugrian languages other than Hungarian, although only remotely connected, still stand in closer relationship to one another than to Hungarian, the relationship between Hungarian and these languages must be very distant indeed.

All this suggests that the Finno-Ugrian languages must have undergone a separation and diffusion at a much earlier date than is generally thought and the fact that leaving the Hungarians aside, they now find themselves in a comparatively confined area, may well be a post-diffusion phenomenon, produced by these peoples being pushed together by external forces after a long period of separation. There are also linguistic indications that all these peoples may have lived in a reasonable proximity to the Caucasus and even Mesopotamia at an earlier stage.[39]

Having regard to the extremely conservative character of the Hungarian language — witnessed by the fact that it has lost practically none of its stock and qualities over the last thousand years[40] — and the very meagre relationship between Hungarian and the Finnish branch of the Finno-Ugrian languages, it appears that the era when Hungarian acquired its scant common vocabulary with these languages must have been not later than 10,000 B.C. and indeed, may have been much earlier. This, of course, does not postulate any ethnic relationship between the Magyars and the peoples now speaking Finnish languages. After all, Hungarian also exhibits some connections with the languages of the Lapps and Samoyeds, yet there is absolutely no ethnic relationship between the Hungarians and these two peoples.[41] One might as well seek to establish a common descent for Englishmen and Albanians on the ground that their languages belong to the same family!

Comparative linguistics therefore afford no valid basis for assuming any substantial ethnic connection between Hungarians on the one hand and Finns, Estonians and their relatives on the other. If any such connection exists, proof of it must be sought in the field of anthropology and not in linguistics. Even if anthropology shows some such connection — to which we shall return below — the high degree of dissimilarity between the languages in question proves conclusively the extremely remote nature of any ethnic relationship.

This leaves us with the Voguls and Ostyaks who, with the Hungarians, are said to form the Ugrian branch of the Finno-Ugrian group. Because the languages of these peoples exhibit closer affinities with Hungarian than the other Finno-Ugrian languages, they are considered as providing the 'missing link' between Hungarians and Finno-Ugrians both from the linguistic and the ethnic points of view. They thus occupy a key position in the Finno-Ugrian ethnic theory, for if it can be shown that they are ethnically not Finno-Ugrians but acquired their languages from contact with other peoples, then the theory of the Finno-Ugrian origin of the Magyars is considerably weakened, if not altogether destroyed.

We have already referred to Wiklund's view that the Voguls and Ostyaks are ethnically not Finno-Ugrians. More recently, a similar opinion has been expressed by the Finnish scholar Vuorela.[42] The difficulty in showing any anthropological connection between these peoples and other peoples with Finno-Ugrian languages is generally recognised. The Voguls and Ostyaks show strong mongoloid features which cannot be found either among the Magyars or other peoples classed as Finno-Ugrians. Sauvageot has sought to explain these mongoloid traits by sug-

Satchel-cover from Bezdéd, Hungary. 9th century

Ladies' ornament from Rakamaz, Hungary. 9th century

Satchel-cover from Galgóc, Hungary. 9th century

gesting that the Voguls and Ostyaks have mixed with Turkic races to the point of losing their original racial characteristics.[43] However, there are two serious objections to this theory. Firstly, there is simply no historical or linguistic evidence of such Turkic-Vogul-Ostyak mixing either in recent times or at any stage in the past. Secondly, the cultural and social gap between Voguls and Ostyaks on the one hand and Turks on the other is so enormous that a Turkic people would hardly have condescended to mix with them.[44]

A Hungarian anthropologist, Paul Lipták, carried out a detailed examination of skulls found in Hungarian graves of the Conquest period and compared them with cranial measurements of Voguls and Ostyaks. It is clear from his report that he approached his investigations with preconceived notions concerning the Ugrian ethnic origin of the Hungarians. Nevertheless, all he could find was that the extreme Europoid Ostyak skulls showed a similarity with the extreme Mongoloid (Sibirid) Hungarian skulls. In other words, when he compared an atypical Hungarian skull with an atypical Ostyak skull, he was able to establish a certain degree of similarity. With the Voguls who are linguistically closer to the Hungarians than the Ostyaks, even such an atypical relationship could not be established.[45]

Lipták also made some significant findings concerning the typological classification of the old Hungarian skulls examined. The so-called Sibirid type, which he regarded as characteristic of the Voguls and Ostyaks, could not be found in its pure form among the Hungarian skulls but only with a fairly strong admixture of proto-Europoid racial characteristics. Even such mixed cranial types formed a minority. The overwhelming majority of the skulls exhibited Turkic characteristics.

It is, of course, obvious that a comparison of atypical elements among any two given peoples is entirely useless, as such elements are clearly the result of outside racial influences. We must therefore regard Lipták's findings as quite conclusively negativing any anthropological relationship between Hungarians on the one hand and Voguls and Ostyaks on the other.

It may be argued, however, that even though an ethnic relationship between Hungarians and Voguls and Ostyaks cannot be established, the affinities between their languages show that they must have lived in close proximity over an extended period. We would not quarrel with this but there is nothing to show that such cohabitation took place within the suggested Finno-Ugrian *Urheimat* or that the Magyars now in the Carpathian Basin ever had anything to do with these two peoples.

It is necessary to point out at this stage how insignificant in numbers the Voguls and Ostyaks are. According to latest statistics, Vogul is spoken by 6,000 persons and Ostyak by 19,000.[47] Even if they are now on the way to extinction and were previously more numerous, their numbers do not appear to have been substantially greater when they were found in a comparatively undisturbed state in the thirteenth century. They must therefore always have consisted of very small populations dispersed over a large area and pursuing a simple hunting and fishing way of life. A change of language for such kind of peoples is not a unique phenomenon and is generally accepted in the case of the Lapps and Samoyeds. It is quite likely that the Voguls and Ostyaks, too, abandoned their original language or languages — the two are still so closely related today that they may be considered dialects of the same language[48] — through contact with a branch of the proto-Hungarians in the distant past.

Indeed, the languages of the Ob-Ugrians still preserve the memory of such a contact, for they have words related to horse-breeding, whilst possessing no horses themselves. Their myths and sagas also refer to horses but possession of these is reserved for the gods and heroes.[49] The Voguls and Ostyaks therefore must have acquired their words connected with the horse from a people superior to them, engaged in horsebreeding, and since those words have their exact parallels in Hungarian, that people must have been the proto-Hungarians or a branch of them.

We have repeatedly referred to a 'branch' of the proto-Hungarians because present-day Hungarians, in spite of their extremely heavy ethnic losses in the course of their wanderings and their turbulent history in the Carpathian Basin, still outnumber the Ob-Ugrians 500:1 so that it would only have required a comparatively small branch of the ancient Magyars to lend their language to the Voguls and Ostyaks. (It is worth thinking about that if these small peoples had come into close contact with the entire body of Hungarians, they would have been completely absorbed by them and would not exist today.)

Indeed, we know of past separations of the Hungarian ethnic body, for, as we have already seen, two substantial branches of the Magyars survived in Transcaucasia and Bashkiria respectively for centuries, although they were geographically far less protected than their brothers in the Carpathian Basin. It is therefore quite likely that a similar separation took place at a much earlier age and a branch of the Hungarians, swept away later by the constant turbulence of peoples in that region, moved into the neighbourhood of the Voguls and Ostyaks — then living perhaps further to the south — and gave its language to them.

The question now remains as to the period in which such transfer of language might have taken place. Peter Hajdu, who puts the date of separation between Hungarians and Ob-Ugrians at about 500 B.C., makes the surprising statement that the rate of evolution of the Hungarian language during the following fifteen hundred years must have been 'strikingly conspicuous in comparison with the linguistic development of the Ugric period', because 'the Hungarian language of the eleventh century can be fairly well understood with a knowledge of modern Hungarian but a Hungarian of the Conquest period could not have made himself understood to an ancestor of Ugric times'. He explains that 'this is due to the fact that the Hungarian language has undergone fewer substantial changes during the last thousand years than it had during the thousand years following its separation from the Ob-Ugric branches'.[50] He therefore postulates a language which is slow in its development during its 'Ugric period', then undergoes revolutionary changes for the next fifteen hundred years and thereafter slows down again for a thousand years, although exposed to a series of substantial linguistic influences in its new habitat. This simply does not make sense and the obvious answer is that the date when contact ceased between the Hungarians and the Ob-Ugrians, quite arbitrarily fixed by Hajdu and others as 500 B.C., must have been very much earlier. Indeed, some scholars have realised this and Bárczi puts the

same date at 1000 B.C.[51] whilst László considers that the separation must have taken place about two thousand five hundred
years before the Conquest period, that is, around 1600 B.C.[52]
Having regard to the highly conservative nature of the Hungarian language, a characteristic which is possessed to a probably
much greater degree by Vogul and Ostyak, even these dates may
be unrealistically late and it appears more likely that the Hungarian and Ob-Ugrian contacts occurred around 2000 B.C.,
which coincides with a period of great upheavals in the Mesopotamian area.

The relationship between the languages of the Hungarians
and the Ob-Ugrians, distant as it is, is therefore a secondary
phenomenon and has no bearing on the ethnic formation of the
Hungarians.

We may now turn to the question of the Hungarians found
near Bashkiria in the thirteenth century. According to the Finno-
Ugrian ethnic theory, these represent the Magyars who remained behind in their original ancestral home. If this is correct,
then one would expect some references to this Bashkirian homeland in the early chronicles and sagas of the Magyars in present-
day Hungary. However, such references are conspicuously
absent. There is no suggestion even of the remotest kind either
in Hungarian or foreign sources that the Hungarians ever lived
in the Bashkirian region or anywhere near it. When the monk
Julian went to look for the eastern Magyars in the thirteenth
century, he was searching for them in the Caucasian region and
only turned north when he found out about the Hungarians
living there by sheer coincidence.[53] These northern Hungarians
were completely lost and forgotten at that time.

On the other hand, it is recorded by Constantinus Porphyrogenetus that in the tenth century, the Hungarians in the Carpathian Basin still exchanged regular messages with their
relatives south of the Caucasus (see Chapter 2). There is a
reasonable inference from this that the Hungarians in the west
regarded these Transcaucasian Hungarians as remaining in their
original homeland and were simply 'writing home'. Similar contacts with the Bashkirian Hungarians were completely lacking.

We have also seen the very clear statement in Kézai's Gesta

and other sources, including some foreign chronicles, that the ancestral home of the Hungarians was in the region of Persia. This location is so far distant from Bashkiria that a confusion of areas cannot be supposed.

Through an analysis of early foreign sources, we have also traced the movement of the Hungarians from the Caucasus to the Carpathian Basin. Many of these sources would have to be ignored or falsified in order to render the Bashkirian homeland acceptable.

Occasionally, attempts have been made to adduce archaeological evidence in support of the Bashkirian homeland of the Hungarians by attributing the so-called Ananyino and Pianobor cultures to them.[54] These cultures which follow one another and extend from about 700 B.C. to about 500 A.D., reflect a fairly simple way of life in which the horse played a very minor role. Yet only three hundred years later when the Hungarians make their definite appearance on the Lower Danube, they are fierce horsemen, a steppe-people to the hilt. Considering their earlier appearances north and even south of the Caucasus which can only be explained by extreme mobility necessitating heavy reliance on the horse, the Pianobor-people — if they were Hungarians — would have had to undergo a revolutionary change in the fifth century A.D., turning them overnight from a simple sedentary people into semi-nomadic horsemen. Quite apart from the inherent improbability of such a sudden transformation, there is no archaeological evidence of such a change. The Pianobor culture ends abruptly in about 500 A.D. without any significant change in its character. Tallgren attributes this sudden end — although somewhat hesitatingly — to the migration of the Magyars to the south and the Ostyaks and Voguls to the north.[55] There are two basic objections to this assumption. Firstly, as we have already seen, the separation of the Magyars and the Ob-Ugrians must have taken place very much earlier. Consequently, if the Voguls and Ostyaks were still in the Pianobor region around 500 A.D., the Magyars just could not have been there. Secondly, the Magyars did not disappear from the area until the end of the thirteenth century. Up till then, they were present in substantial numbers as the placenames of Hungarian origin

41

indicate.[56] Consequently, it is much more likely that the sudden end of the Pianobor culture, far from being connected with the departure of the Magyars, signifies the arrival of their northern branch in that area, wiping out or dislodging the primitive settlements existing there. This accords with the view of a number of historians that the branch of the Hungarians living near Bashkiria migrated there with the Volga Bulgars about the seventh century A.D.[57]

As already stated in Chapter 2, these northern Hungarians were probably the White Ugors or Saragurs, who were first to leave the Transcaucasian homeland of the Hungarians and whose memory gradually disappeared. They represent an interesting, if sad, episode in the ethnic history of the Hungarians but furnish no support for the Finno-Ugrian ethnic theory.

The Finno-Ugrian ethnic theory is therefore left with the slender relationship between Hungarian and the Finnish branch of languages as its sole supportable argument. We have already expressed the view that this cannot furnish a sound basis for the assertion of any ethnic relationship. Indeed, the German ethnologist and prehistorian Haensell has come out strongly against the assumption of a Finno-Ugrian *Urvolk* or common ethnic stock on the basis of linguistic affinities.[58] It stands to reason that the slight similarities shown by these languages may well have come about through contacts between ethnically different peoples in the distant past. Even if these contacts eventually resulted in some ethnic connection through intermarriage, the extremely remote nature of linguistic relationship indicates that such connection must have ceased such a long time ago that it cannot throw any real light on the origin or prehistory of the Hungarians.

The feeling of remoteness created by comparative linguistics and examination of other arguments of the Finno-Ugrian theory, is more than backed up by the findings of other disciplines relevant to the study of prehistory. Thus, supposedly Finno-Ugrian elements are either hardly discernible or totally non-existent in Hungarian folklore,[59] music[60] and archaeological finds.[61] Even when some writers report discovery of some such elements — and such reports have been rare — one is tempted to ask whether

42

such 'discovery' is not the product of preconceived notions attributing a Finno-Ugrian origin to cultural elements atypical of Hungarians or simple artifacts common to certain primitive occupations all over Eurasia.

Over the last fifty years, attempts have been made by the Hungarian anthropologists Bartucz,[62] Nemeskéri[63] and Lipták[64] to find an anthropological basis for the Finno-Ugrian ethnic theory. Their researches have indeed established the existence of two major ethnic types among the Magyar conquerors. One of these which was more characteristic of poorer graves of the Conquest period and was in any event in the minority, was classified by Bartucz as belonging to the East Baltic racial type and he therefore assumed that this represented the Ugric element among the Hungarians. More recent studies by Lipták, however, show that this type among the early Hungarian skulls has a more composite and complicated character. In any event, the so-called East Baltic type is well-represented not only among some members of the Finnish group of peoples but also among Latvians, Lithuanians and even Slavic populations in eastern and north-eastern Europe. This anthropological type is therefore not confined to Finno-Ugrian peoples, nor are Finno-Ugrian peoples predominantly of this type,[65] and even if it can be regarded as more characteristic of the early Finnish and related tribes, than their present-day successors, its origins — like those of all anthropological types — go back well before the beginnings of ethnic formations resulting in the various peoples of the world as we know them today.[66]

The significant finding of anthropologists concerning the early Magyars, therefore, is not that one of their racial types bears some relationship to Finno-Ugrian types but that they consisted of two distinct ethnic strains. This duality, of course, is clearly stated in the Nimrod-legend (Chapter 1) and the real question which we now intend to investigate is who these two peoples were the merger of which made up the Hungarian nation.

CHAPTER 4

A Race of Turks

'The Magyars are a race of Turks,' writes the early tenth century Arab geographer, Ibn Rusta.[1] Another Arab, Mahmud Gardezi, writing about 1050 but quoting from a source dating from around 913, repeats this and adds, 'These Magyars are a handsome people and of good appearance and their clothes are of silk brocade and their weapons are of silver and are encrusted with gold'.[2]

We have already seen that when the Magyars are first clearly identified in Byzantine literature, they are repeatedly referred to as Turks (Chapter 2). That this term was not a mere misnomer but was based on the general appearance, customs, social and political organisation and martial habits of the Magyars of that period, is clear from the various descriptions given by ninth and tenth century Byzantine writers.[3]

These Arab and Byzantine descriptions were so fundamentally different from the humble origins attributed to the Magyars by the protagonists of the Finno-Ugrian theory and were so irreconcilable with the way of life of the Ob-Ugrians, that Hungarian historians of the nineteenth century treated the Finno-Ugrian line promoted by the linguists with considerable reservations.[4] Indeed, László Szalay in his definitive *History of Hungary* published in 1852, firmly declared that Hungarians were a 'Turkish nation', which originally resided in Central Asia, between the Altai Mountains and the Caspian Sea.[5] Henrik Marczali, writing in the *History of the Hungarian Nation*, published in 1895 to commemorate the first millenium of the Magyars in the Carpathian Basin, declared that the tradition of relationship between Hungarians and Huns was based on 'healthy historical sense' and asserted that investigations as to the origins of a language, although important, did not throw light on the origins of a nation. He regarded the early Hungarians as a Turkish-Ugrian mixture, with the Turks as the dominant element.[6]

A Race of Turks

This Turkish leaning of Hungarian historians received considerable impetus from the writings of Armin Vámbéry, a noted Hungarian orientalist, who devoted a lifetime to demonstrating a cultural and ethnic as well as linguistic relationship between Turks and Magyars.

In his principal work, *Der Ursprung der Magyaren* (Leipzig, 1882), Vámbéry pointed out the Turkish etymologies of Hungarian personal, tribal and clan names found in Byzantine and mediaeval Hungarian sources and after dealing in some detail with the Turkish aspects of ancient Hungarian culture, customs, military tactics and social and political organisation, devoted some two hundred pages to a careful analysis of the Turkish features of the Hungarian language. He asserted that the phonetics, grammatical relationships and vocabulary of Hungarian were all closer to the Turco-Tartar languages than to the Finno-Ugrian group and maintained that almost two-thirds of the Hungarian vocabulary was more intimately connected with Turkish and could be better explained etymologically from the latter than from the Finno-Ugrian languages. He argued that Hungarian words of Turkish origin were not loanwords but that Hungarian had a double or mixed character, as a result of which it could be equally classified as a Finno-Ugrian or a Turco-Tartar language.

Vámbéry stressed that the Turkish elements in the Hungarian language were so deep-seated and of such basic nature that they could not have been acquired by subjugation and cultural influence on the part of a Turkish people, but postulated an intensive mixing between a Turkish and a Finno-Ugrian people at an early stage of Hungarian prehistory. As to the ethnic origin of Hungarians, he considered them a basically Turkish people which came into extended contact with Finno-Ugrians, resulting in an 'ethnic amalgam' in which the Turks remained the culturally, socially and politically dominant element.

These propositions of Vámbéry were violently attacked by Hunfalvy, Budenz, Szinnyei and other members of the Finno-Ugrian school. Due to the preoccupation of that era with the study of linguistics in the field of prehistory, the controversy mainly raged on a linguistic level and the very important non-linguistic considerations raised by Vámbéry were largely ignored. Whilst Vámbéry may have been himself to blame, at least partly, for this trend in the dispute, as he had clearly attempted to attack the linguists on their home territory, it is nevertheless much to be regretted that his numerous non-linguistic arguments supporting the Turkish ethnic origin of the Magyars were simply swept aside. As it happened, the linguists carried the day and the Hungarian Academy of Sciences lent its complete support to the protagonists of the Finno-Ugrian ethnic theory (see Chapter 3).

Truth, however, shows a strange resilience at times and some twenty years after Vámbéry seemed to have been well and truly defeated, some of his propositions received cautious support from an unexpected quarter. Zoltán Gombocz, an eminent Hungarian linguist of the Finno-Ugrian school, published a treatise in 1912[7] in which he analysed the Turkish loanwords in the Hungarian language. He concluded that approximately two hundred and thirty basic words relating to domestic animals and animal husbandry, agriculture, buildings and household equipment, trade utensils and handicrafts, clothing and wearing apparel, social and political institutions and relations, parts of the human body, illnesses, religion, writing, numerals, time, nature, hunting and fishing, plants and the animal world and also a number of verbs of everyday use, had been borrowed from a Turkic language closely akin to that of the Volga Bulgars, the present-day Chuvash.

He observed, however, that the language perpetuated by these loanwords was not the same as that of the Volga Bulgars but was a language now extinct which only survived in the loanwords preserved in Hungarian.[8] We shall later return to this finding as it is of immense significance in tracing the ancestry of the Magyars.

Gombocz demonstrated the great antiquity of this Turkish stratum in Hungarian by showing analogous phonetic changes undergone by both true Hungarian words and the adopted Turkic vocabulary.

Gombocz further noted that the Hungarian verb roots which agreed with Turco-Bulgar verb roots had been taken over with-

46

out the addition of any Hungarian suffixes, contrary to Hungarian verbs borrowed from Latin, German and various Slavic languages.[9] He explained this phenomenon with phonetic and morphological correspondences between Hungarian and Old Turkic,[10] but this explanation was not universally accepted and at least one writer has since suggested the bilingualism of the ancient Magyars (already noted by Constantinus Porphyrogenetus) as the true cause for the natural acceptance of these Turkic verbs in Hungarian.[11]

Gombocz originally did not draw any conclusions from his findings which could have offended the Finno-Ugrian school and ascribed the adoption of the Old Turkic vocabulary analysed by him to mere cultural relations without any intensive mixing of populations.[12] Later on, however, he turned to a study of the Hungarian national traditions relating to the brotherhood of Huns and Magyars and attributing these to contacts with the Turco-Bulgars, concluded that elements of the latter must have contributed to the ethnic formation of the early Hungarians, resulting in a fusion of two races. He suggested that this amalgamation had taken place in the Caucasian region in the fifth, sixth and seventh centuries A.D. and sought to support his theory by the presence of Alan loanwords in Hungarian.[13]

These conclusions of Gombocz were rightly hailed by Hóman as 'marking the end of the exclusive reign of Finno-Ugrian linguistics in the field of Hungarian prehistory'.[14] Although he had started out as a Finno-Ugrian linguist himself, Gombocz clearly laid the linguistic foundations for a new school of Hungarian prehistory which declared with increasing boldness the Turkish ethnic affiliations of the Magyars.

The breakthrough was achieved nearly twenty years later by Gyula Németh, the eminent Hungarian Turcologist. In his work *A honfoglaló magyarság kialakulása* (Budapest, 1930), Németh dealt exhaustively with the role played by the Turco-Bulgars in the formation of the early Hungarians. He stressed the significance of Turco-Bulgar loanwords in Hungarian and, after pointing out several historical data regarding the stay of the Magyars in the Caucasian homeland of the Bulgars, confirmed in many respects by early Hungarian chronicles and the national tradi-

47

tion, he embarked on a detailed analysis of the tribal system and tribe names of the Magyars of the Conquest period. He concluded that the Hungarian people resulted from an amalgamation between one large Finno-Ugrian and six to eight smaller Turkish tribes which came about prior to the sixth century A.D. In his opinion, the Turkish element had the dominant role in the organisation and leadership of the people so formed.

These views, which Németh had already expressed in some of his earlier writings, were received with great satisfaction by Hungarian public opinion which had always been lukewarm towards the Finno-Ugrian theory.[15] The Magyars were by instinct more attracted to the martial Turks than the humble Ugrian relatives foisted on them by the linguists. The new doctrine of dual descent of Hungarians was adopted with equal enthusiasm by historians (although for more scientific reasons)[16] and even Géza Bárczi, the eminent Hungarian linguist, conceded that 'from the ethnic point of view [the Magyars] became strongly mixed with Turkish elements, so that . . . around the time of the conquest of their actual country, the Finno-Ugrian kernel was perhaps no more than a minority'.[17]

The intervening forty-odd years have brought little change in the basic essentials of this new theory and it is now generally accepted that a Turkish people or peoples contributed strongly to the ethnic formation of the early Hungarians, resulting in a people of dual ancestry.[18] The location of the ethnic melting pot in which this fusion of two races took place has been the subject of much speculation, being put by different writers in various places ranging from Central Asia to the middle Volga and the Caucasus. All these theories were based on conjecture and none of them has found universal acceptance. It is worth noting, however, that the leading contemporary Hungarian prehistorian, Gyula László, has come out increasingly strongly in favour of a Caucasian *Urheimat*, at least as regards the Turkish component of the Hungarian people.[19]

The period and duration of the Turco-Ugrian ethnogenesis has also been variously estimated but the general tendency has been to lengthen its duration and to put its commencement further and further back in point of time. A recent work by two Hungarian linguists, Loránd Benkö and Samu Imre, suggests that it probably lasted a thousand years and took place between the fifth century B.C. and the fifth century A.D.[20]

It is interesting to note that the doctrine of formation of the early Magyars from a fusion of Finno-Ugrian and Turkish elements is still strongly based on linguistic study, although historical data and the national tradition are also invoked in its support. There are many other indications, however, pointing to the important and probably dominant role played by a Turkish people in the ethnic formation of Hungarians. It may be now useful to review these briefly.

Anthropological studies of grave finds from the Conquest period in Hungary, carried out by Bartucz, Nemeskéri and Lipták, have demonstrated that the numerically strongest element among the Magyar conquerors was of the Turanid type, a racial type characteristic of Turkish peoples.[21] According to Bartucz, this element comprised at least 35 to 40 per cent of the early Hungarians. All three authors mentioned agree that people of the Turanid type formed the leading social stratum of the Hungarian conquerors. Recent studies by Lipták have also shown that this leading Hungarian stratum was anthropologically related to the leading classes of the Volga Bulgars in the tenth century.[22] It is not irrelevant to note that this racial type is still fairly dominant among present-day Hungarians and is generally regarded as the true 'Hungarian type'.[23]

We have already referred to the conclusion long accepted by historians that the social and political organisation and military tactics of the early Hungarians were characteristic of a Turkish people. More recently, Ferenc Eckhart has established by a careful analysis of old Hungarian legal customs and institutions, some of which have survived into the twentieth century, that these, too, were typical of the culture of Turkish peoples in the second half of the first millenium.[24]

Hungarian folklore and ethnography show predominantly old Turkish elements.[25] This is true even of present-day Hungarian folklore, which suggests that what we are dealing with here is not a mere survival of borrowed cultural motifs but the continued cultural activity of a living people. Archaeological finds testify to a remarkable similarity between the funerary customs, weapons and ornaments of the Magyars of the Conquest period and the Volga Bulgars.[26] To a lesser degree, these finds are also similar to the relics of Huns, Avars and Khazars which are all generally accepted as peoples of Turkish origin.[27]

Several characters of the old Hungarian script, preserved by the Szekelys of Transylvania, are identical with the inscriptions of the Altai Turks dating from the sixth and seventh centuries A.D.[28]

The most ancient stratum of Hungarian folk music is, in its construction, methods and types of melodies, intimately connected with the musical traditions of Turkish peoples.[29] It may be safely stated that the musical idiom of the Hungarians is basically Turkish.[30] (This is conceded even by those who think they can discern faint traces of a 'Ugrian' stratum in Hungarian folk music.)[31] It is significant that the only Finno-Ugrian people whose music shows any substantial similarity with Hungarian folk songs are the Tsheremiss and they have been under the cultural influence of the Chuvash (the descendants of the Volga Bulgars) over a considerable period.[32]

Lastly, returning again to linguistic considerations, there is the well-established fact that in addition to their 'proper language' the Hungarian conquerors also spoke a Turkic idiom. This idiom which, as the bilingual use of old Turkic names suggests, was still understood by the Hungarian upper classes in the second half of the tenth century and perhaps even a century later,[33] was clearly the same Turkic language of which Gombocz discovered some two hundred and thirty words in present-day Hungarian. These words then cannot be regarded as 'loanwords' from an ethnic point of view, since they represent the patrimony of a people which merged with the 'Ugrian' branch of the ancient Hungarians and formed a substantial part of the nation so born.

As Gombocz has demonstrated, the old Turkic language from which these words were derived, was not the same as the language of the Volga Bulgars but was another variant related to the former. Consequently, in spite of the similarities between the

early culture, social and political organisation and customs of
the Magyar conquerors and the Volga Bulgars, the ancient Hungarians — or more specifically, the Turkish element among them
— cannot be regarded as a branch of the Volga Bulgars but
merely as a related but different people.

This view is confirmed by the rôle played by the wives of the
sons of Belar in the Nimrod-legend (see Chapter 1). Assuming,
as most historians do, that Belar represents the Bulgars or one
of their branches, his people must have been clearly different
from the Hungarians at the time of the events symbolised by the
mythical rape. This part of the Hungarian national tradition
therefore indicates that the Turkish component of the Magyar
people could not have been identical with the Bulgars, although
it was most likely ethnically related to them.

It now remains to find out who these Turkish Hungarians
really were.

CHAPTER 5

The Hun Brothers

The Huns made a definite and traumatic entry into history when they crossed the Volga and invaded Southern Russia under their king Balamber around 375 A.D. Their meteoric rise, brilliant but savage campaigns and sudden collapse following Attila's death in 453 are only too well known. The contemporary 'news media', the Western and Byzantine chroniclers, have left us ample, although highly prejudiced, records of their exploits in the West. Much less is known about them in the East.

Most historians agree that the Huns previously lived in Central Asia, on the borders of the Chinese empire. There are several references in ancient Chinese sources suggestive of their presence. The sage Mencius, writing in the second half of the fourth century B.C., mentions a people called Hiun-yu. Other ancient Chinese texts which go back to the eighth century B.C., contain several references to Hien-yun and Huen-yu. Later on, still centuries before the Christian era, the name Hiung-nu makes its appearance. All these names are applied to fierce, nomadic horsemen in Inner Mongolia and its surrounding regions who formed and re-formed themselves into huge empires and were constantly embattling the Chinese. Eventually, the Great Wall of China was built to keep them out.[1]

Whether the people or peoples described by the Chinese under these various names were identical with the Huns has not been established beyond doubt. It is clear, however, that they were Turks. Chinese sources depict them as men with large prominent noses and strong beards[2] and according to Chinese dynastic histories, they spoke a Turkish language.[3] Archaeological investigations by Soviet scientists of graves in the Altai region show a large number of brachycephalic heads occurring since about 1200 B.C. which later reappear in Khwarezm and near the Aral Sea, and can be found again during the period of

52

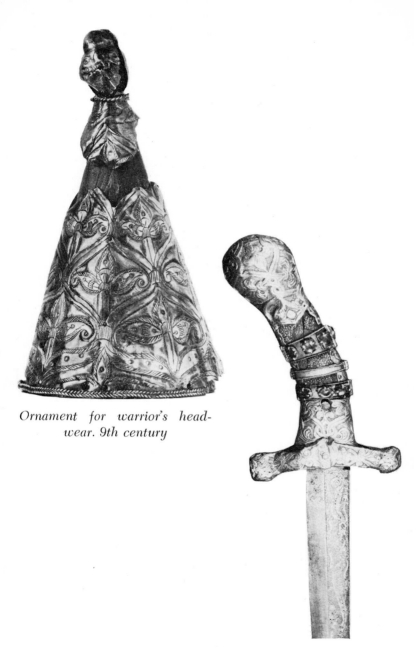

Ornament for warrior's head-wear. 9th century

Ceremonial sword of Hungarian ruler. 9th century

Gold drinking vessel from Treasure of Nagyszentmiklós, Hungary. 10th century

Gold fruit-plate from Treasure of Nagyszentmiklós, Hungary, 10th century

Hunnish occupation of the Great Hungarian Plain.[4] It is significant that these brachycephalic grave finds in the Altai region
are surrounded by an almost exclusively dolichocephalic milieu.[5]

Archaeological comparisons of fibulas, belts, weapons and
other objects found in graves show a remarkable unity of culture
between the regions where the Hiung-nu once lived and the
areas where the Huns later make their appearance. This is particularly attested by the striking similarity of the so-called 'animal
art' in all these finds.[6]

Between 158 and 166 A.D., the Huns are mentioned in Chinese
sources under their proper name as a people which have been
driven out of western Mongolia and eastern Turkestan by the
northern branch of the Hiung-nu and forced to move to the
western part of Turkestan.[7]

There is therefore ample evidence of a crucible of Turkish
peoples to the north and north-west of China from which the
Huns emerge towards the middle of the second century of our
era to commence their westward push which brings them to the
Volga at around 375.

In a rare moment of unanimity, virtually all historians agree
that the Huns were Turks and spoke an Old Turkic dialect.[8]

The Huns whose westward movement we have traced in broad
outline, however, were not the only members of their race to
appear on the pages of history. In his *Geography* written around
the middle of the second century A.D., Ptolemy speaks of Huns
living between the Bastarnas and Roxolans. His description of
the habitations of the two adjoining nations places these Huns
in western Ciscaucasia, near the upper reaches of the Kuban
river and in the region east of the Sea of Azov.[9] Their settlements probably extended to the south-western banks of the
lower Don.[10]

The presence of Huns in the region of the lower Don after the
middle of the second century is also confirmed by the notorious
legend concerning their origin from relations between Scythian
witches and devils, which is recorded by Jordanes in his *Getica*
and can be traced to Gothic myths dating from the period in
question.[11]

These Huns were living in the neighbourhood of Iranian tribes subsequently identified as Alans, and their close connections with the latter are attested by the fact that both Huns and Alans keep cropping up as mercenaries in the Armenian army from the end of the third century.[12] The Huns, however, lived further to the south than the Alans and the area occupied by them clearly included portions of the Caucasus and, indeed, reached down into Transcaucasia. This is confirmed by Orosius and Ammianus who state that prior to attacking the Goths in 375, the Huns lived in 'inaccessible mountains' — which could only mean the Caucasus[13] — and also by the occurrence of Turkic names in the Caucasian region and archaeological finds in excavations near Gori in Georgia, the Iberia of old.[14]

Attacks by the Caucasian Huns against Persian territories are mentioned in contemporary sources from around 230 onwards, followed by alternating wars and alliances between Huns and Persians right through the third and fourth centuries.[15] The presence of Huns in the Persian army besieging Dura-Europos (in Syria) shortly after the middle of the third century is suggested by several Turkic names and designations on Persian *ostraka* (pieces of pottery with writing on them) found in the area.[16]

Armenian historical writings refer to wars between Huns and Armenians in the southern Caucasus as early as during the reign of Valarsaces (149-127 B.C.). Certain powerful fortifications in the Caucasian province of Albania, then Armenian territory, are repeatedly mentioned in early Armenian sources by the name of 'the Hun gates', the defence of which was entrusted to particularly reliable Armenian warriors. Huns appear as allies of the kings of Armenia from 227 A.D. onwards and Armenian sources make several references to them in the third and fourth centuries.[17] Although none of the Armenian histories in question is earlier than the fourth century A.D., and some were written at a considerably later date, their testimony cannot be disregarded.

These Caucasian Huns were clearly an advance party of the main body of the Huns which appeared at the Volga around 375.[18] Consequently, they must have been separated from their Central Asian brothers for centuries. There is, however, nothing unusual about parts of a nomadic people being so far removed from one another in time and space. From the sixth century onwards, Bulgars lived on the middle Volga, in the Caucasian region and in present-day Bulgaria, whilst a few centuries later we find substantial bodies of Hungarians in the Carpathian Basin, in Bashkiria and the neighbourhood of Persia. Similar instances could be given of Avars, Kumans, Petchenegs and other peoples belonging to the Turkish race.

It is now necessary to define the limits of the stay of the Huns in the Caucasian region in point of time. Altheim considers that they moved to the area in company with the Alans towards the end of the second century B.C.[19] The geographical position of these Huns and the early references to them in Armenian sources rather suggest that they may have preceded the Alans by a few years, if not more. In any event, they must have firmly established themselves in the Caucasus by the beginning of the Christian era.

We have no direct evidence of the actual departure of the Huns from the Caucasus. In 450, they are mentioned as assisting the Armenians in their uprising against the Byzantines. In 481, they are the allies of Byzantium in suppressing another Armenian revolt. Between these two dates, in 463 to be exact, the Saragurs, Ugors and Onogurs make their first appearance in the old territory of the Huns between the Caucasus and the Sea of Azov.[20] There is little doubt that these peoples contained strong Hunnish elements; they are repeatedly referred to in Byzantine sources as Huns or as peoples living in the company of Huns. After the end of the fifth century, Huns are no longer mentioned in the Caucasus proper but Byzantine sources continue to refer to them as inhabiting the area near the Sea of Azov and other parts of Southern Russia. At this point of time, the Caucasian Huns appear to lose their identity and their place is taken by the Onogurs, Saragurs, Ugors and Bulgars, all living in the northern Caucasian region and around the lower reaches of the Volga and the Don and moving northwards and westwards by successive waves. All the four peoples mentioned continue to be designated as Huns in various contemporary sources from time to time.

We have already identified the Ugors and Saragurs as two separate branches of the Magyars and the Onogurs as the an-

cestors of the Bulgars (see Chapter 2). Since all these peoples
emerge at the same time and in the same place when and where
the Caucasian Huns suddenly disappear and as a contemporary
records unanimously refer to them as Huns, it is virtually beyond
argument that they represent the descendants of the Huns who
formerly lived in the Caucasus. Indeed, as far as the Onogurs
and Bulgars are concerned, this is accepted by the overwhelming
majority of historians.[21] The same concession is generally not
made concerning the Hungarians; indeed, the contrary is often
asserted. However, in view of the demonstrable fusion of a substantial body of Turco-Bulgars with the 'Ugric' ancestors of the
Magyars (see Chapter 4) and the generally acknowledged
identity of the Turco-Bulgars with the Huns, it seems to the
writer that any objection to the ethnic relationship between
Huns and Hungarians is merely a matter of semantics.

This ethnic relationship is confirmed by the unanimous testimony of early Hungarian and foreign sources and is also supported by the overlapping of the areas which Huns and Magyars
can be shown to have occupied in the Caucasian region between
the second century B.C. and the fifth century A.D.

We can therefore declare without hesitation that the Turks
who impregnated the early Magyars with their racial and cultural characteristics were Huns and that they were the Huns of
the Caucasus.

This Hun-Magyar ethnogenesis must have been an essentially
peaceful process. Gombocz has pointed out that the Turco-
Bulgar loanwords in Hungarian all relate to peaceful activities,
such as animal husbandry, agriculture, domestic implements,
trade and commerce and the like, and there is not a single expression among them connected with warfare.[22] The Magyars
therefore must have voluntarily allied themselves to the Huns
when the latter arrived in the Caucasus, and were thereupon
probably incorporated in the Hunnish political organisation as
one of its constituent bodies with more or less equal rights. This
supposition is entirely consistent with the processes of empire-
building prevalent among horsemen of the steppes at the time.[23]
The legendary brotherhood of Hunor and Magor certainly negatives any suggestion of savage oppression or conquest.

The fusion between Hungarians and part of the Caucasian Huns must have been complete by the end of the fourth century A.D. Soon after that time, we find the Ugors as a completely self-contained people and masters of their own destiny. We have already demonstrated that they were identical with the Magyars who eventually settled in the Carpathian Basin (Chapter 2). There seems little doubt that by the time the Ugors emerged north of the Caucasus in the fifth century, the Hunnish element among them was completely amalgamated with the rest and the entire people spoke Hungarian. This is confirmed by the fact that this Hun-Magyar amalgam was able to produce an offshoot in Bashkiria, the language of which was still pure Hungarian in the thirteenth century.

Furthermore, the fact that the name Ugor occurs in a composite form in the names of other peoples making their appearance at the same time, namely the Saragurs and the Onogurs, and that it keeps recurring as a suffix in the names of other Hunnish fragments, such as the Kutrigurs and Altiogurs, during the next two centuries, suggests that prior to the dissipation of the Caucasian Huns, the people identified as Ugor achieved a degree of pre-eminence among them and possibly provided leaders and upper classes for the others. To be called an Ugor, then, was a mark of distinction for these Huns even while they were still inhabiting their Caucasian territories and when they left there, this was the name they adopted in place of their original designation. Such a change of name is again entirely in accordance with the practices of Turkic and related peoples of which several instances can be given.[24]

The ancient town of Gori on the river Kur in Transcaucasia in the vicinity of which archaeological finds have been unearthed suggesting the presence of the Huns there early in the Christian era (see above), was probably the focal point of this Ugor territory and its very name appears to represent an earlier form of Ugor.

Further proof of completion of the Hun-Magyar ethnogenesis by the end of the fourth century is furnished by the Szekelys of Transylvania. This branch of Hungarians which occupies the valleys of the south-eastern Carpathians and adjoining areas of

Transylvania and also has substantial colonies in the Rumanian Regat,[25] including Bucharest itself, numbers close to one million. According to the earliest Hungarian chronicles and the own traditions of the Szekelys themselves, they were already living in Transylvania when the Hungarians arrived there and joined the latter of their own accord. The historical truth of this assertion is accepted by even such sceptics as Macartney.[26]

These early chronicles and the traditions of the Szekelys also assert that they were the descendants of Attila's Huns who remained behind after the collapse of the Hunnish empire. There are also foreign mediaeval sources containing similar statements.[27] Whilst this aspect of the Szekelys' descent has not found general acceptance, there is nothing inherently improbable in it.

Most modern students of the subject agree that the Szekelys had a Turkish culture and tribal organisation.[28] However, the strange fact remains that their tribe and clan names were definitely of Hungarian origin.[29] Furthermore, there is no evidence that they ever spoke any other language but Hungarian. If they had spoken a Turkic or other non-Hungarian dialect at the time of their adhesion to the Magyars at the end of the ninth century, surely their language would have survived long enough among the mountains of Transylvania to be noted by some mediaeval chronicler. Given their substantial numbers and the sheltered position of their habitations, one would have expected their language to remain in use up to modern times. However, there is no trace of a separate Szekely language whatever.[30]

In inquiring into the original language of the Szekelys, we are also assisted by their alphabet. The Szekelys had their own system of writing from early times which they preserved well into the seventeenth century. This script was perfectly adapted to Hungarian phonetics and had separate characters for every sound in the Hungarian language.

The Szekely alphabet and corresponding modern Hungarian characters

It will be readily seen that whereas the modern Hungarian writing, based on the Latin alphabet, has to employ composite consonants to render various Hungarian phonemes (cs, gy, ly, ny, sz, ty, zs), the Szekely alphabet had a single character for each. Furthermore, there are several characters in the Szekely script for specifically Hungarian sounds, such as gy, ly, ny, ty and zs, which do not exist either in Turkic languages or in Turkic scripts to which the Szekely alphabet is related. It is clear, therefore, that the Szekelys must have acquired their script at a time when they were speaking Hungarian.

The outstanding expert on Szekely script, Gyula Németh, regards it as 'inconceivable' that the Szekelys acquired their alphabet from the Hungarians after the conversion of the latter to Christianity around 1000[31] and we must agree with this. Consequently, even if the Szekelys learnt their system of writing from the Magyars and did not bring it with them from the East, they must have adopted it virtually simultaneously with their union with the Hungarians.[32]

All this suggests that the Szekelys were already speaking Hungarian when they teamed up with the Magyars at the end of the ninth century. Furthermore, as there is no evidence whatever of any intensive contact between these two peoples during the centuries immediately preceding the arrival of the Magyars in the Carpathian Basin, it is a fair conclusion that the Szekelys already spoke Hungarian when they first settled in Transylvania.

Since there is no reason to doubt that the Szekelys came to the Carpathians under the Huns and indeed, the ethnic turbulence created by the westward sweep of the latter furnishes a

59

perfectly plausible explanation for such event, we are further justified in concluding that the Szekelys broke away from the Hun-Magyar amalgam formed in the Caucasian region towards the end of the fourth century. The very fact that they settled in a mountainous region with such ease confirms this conclusion.[33] It follows from the foregoing that they must have been speaking Hungarian at that point of time.

These considerations lead us to the view that a substantial Hungarian-speaking ethnic body must have been fully formed from a fusion of Hun and Magyar tribes in the Caucasus before the end of the fourth century.

Before leaving the Caucasian Huns, there is one more matter of interest we ought to mention. Early Armenian sources contain several references to the town of Hunoracerta in one of the northern provinces of Greater Armenia adjoining the Caucasian Albania.[34] As a learned Armenian priest, Kristóf Lukácsy, writing in Hungary towards the middle of the last century has explained, 'certa' means 'work, building, town' in Armenian and occurs in a composite form in the names of several ancient Armenian towns, such as Carcathiocerta, Semiramocerta, Ervantocerta, Tigranocerta, etc. (town of Carcathios, Semiramis, Ervantes, Tigranes). As to the last one, Plutarch expressly observes that it was founded by Tigranes. Consequently, concludes Lukácsy, Hunoracerta means a town founded by Hunor and he identifies this personage with the mythical ancestor of the Huns in the Nimrod-legend.[35]

According to Gyula Németh, the etymology of Hunor is *hun-eri* (Hun man).[56] Since Hunoracerta was situated within the general area occupied by the Caucasian Huns, Lukácsy's explanation as to its origins must be clearly right, subject to the correction that Hunor was not a person but a branch of the Hun people.

Having identified the elder son of Nimrod as the Caucasian branch of the Huns, we may now turn our attention to the younger son, Magor. Before doing so, however, let us examine a further convincing proof of the Caucasian homeland of the Hungarians: their connections with the Empire of Persia.

CHAPTER 6

The Persian Connection

The question of Persian loanwords in Hungarian has long been neglected by linguists. In a recent definitive work on the Hungarian language, Loránd Benkö only lists three: *vár* (fortress), *vásár* (market) and *vám* (toll, duty). He ascribes these to contacts with Persian merchants who visited the settlements of the Hungarians and declares that 'the forefathers of the Hungarians never lived in the immediate vicinity of Persian territories'.[1]

It is, of course, not immediately obvious why Hungarians should have adopted such words as 'fortress' and 'toll' from Persian merchants. It is much more likely that these words found their way into their language when they were in intensive contact with the Persian Empire, paying toll on entering the border and confronting Persian fortresses facing their territory.

However, the simple fact is that Persian loanwords are much more numerous in Hungarian than the meagre examples given by Benkö. Over a century ago, Lukácsy listed over thirty of which the following seem to be quite convincing: *abroncs* (hoop), *arc* (face), *bárány* (lamb), *dajka* (nurse), *ezer* (thousand), *hab* (foam), *hombár* (granary), *huszár* (hussar, cavalryman), *kincs* (treasure), *kos* (ram), *oroszlán* (lion), *sár* (mud), *seregély* (starling), *som* (cornel), *tárkony* (a medicinal plant), *zeng* (resound).[2]

Writing in 1882, Vámbéry gave twenty Persian loanwords of which some were identical with those contained in Lukácsy's list but there were also several additional ones, such as *ármány* (evil spirit), *bálvány* (idol), *csárda* (inn), *csésze* (cup), *nád* (reed), *pad* (bench), *sárkány* (dragon).[3]

To these, the writer may add another four: *bán* (lord, provincial governor), *garaboly* (woven basket), *kutya* (dog), *satrafa* (domineering person).

Bán is a particularly important word as its meaning is exactly

61

the same in both Persian and Hungarian. The governors of the military provinces protecting the southern frontiers of mediaeval Hungary invariably bore this title and the Viceroy of Croatia was called *bán* right up to 1918. Hungarians therefore must have adopted this word as a political designation at a time when they were in such intimate contact with the Persian Empire that they borrowed the political institutions of the latter.

Satrafa clearly brings to mind the Persian satraps and the secondary meaning acquired by it indicates prolonged hostilities between Hungarians and Persians.

The word *kutya* (dog) is also of some significance as Hungarian contains another word of identical meaning, *eb*, which is of Finno-Ugrian derivation. The fact that Hungarians adopted a second word for the same concept (which is now the word more commonly used) indicates extended relations with the Persians, especially when we consider that several other words relating to animals and plants were also borrowed from them.

The other words listed by Lukácsy and Vámbéry all relate to everyday concepts and in some instances have a cultic significance, *ármány* (evil spirit), *bálvány* (idol), *sárkány* (dragon). *Dajka* (nurse) is a very important word as it indicates a close personal relationship. Words of domestic and economic connotation such as *abroncs* (hoop), *csárda* (inn), *hombár* (granary), are suggestive of intensive co-existence over an extended period.

We can therefore assert with some confidence that the presence of Persian loanwords in Hungarian can only be explained on the basis that these two nations lived side by side over a long period and were in intimate contact with each other. It appears certainly fanciful to attribute these extensive borrowings to mere trading relations with visiting Persian merchants.

Vámbéry makes the interesting observation that Tsheremiss and other Finno-Ugrian languages contain only such Persian loanwords as can be directly traced to Russian or Tartar mediation, whereas the Persian loanwords in Hungarian cannot be so traced and appear to have been acquired through direct contact with the Persians.[4]

An ancient stratum of Persian loanwords in Hungarian was also noted by the eminent Hungarian linguist Bernát Munkácsi and he attributed these to Old Persian, Avesta, Middle Persian and Pamirian influences. The presence of these Persian loan-words, along with other very old loanwords of Caucasian origin, induced Munkácsi to place the ancestral home of the Hungarians in the northern Caucasus.[5]

Linguistics, however, are not the only source from which we can prove the Persian connections of the early Hungarians. The art of the Hungarians of the Conquest period, as witnessed by numerous tenth century finds throughout the Carpathian Basin, bears a strongly Sassanian character. The favourite motif of Sassanian art, the *palmette,* dominates Hungarian art objects of the Conquest period, along with other characteristic Persian ornamental forms, such as the tree of life, the winged lion, dragons, stylised birds of prey and other mythical animals. This is most obvious in early Hungarian gold and silver work which we can classify as purely Sassanian. Indeed, it is not only the outward appearance of this branch of Hungarian art which is dominated by Persian motifs but the technique itself with which these objects have been executed, is typical of Persian gold and silver-smiths of the Sassanian era.[6]

The gold and silver objects thus impregnated with Sassanian art forms and techniques are, nevertheless, truly Hungarian. They consist only of such items as the early Hungarians had use for: ornaments for swords and other weapons, belt buckles, head-dress decorations, drinking vessels, horseriding outfits and personal jewellery.[7] A particularly interesting group is constituted by the silver satchel-covers, often inlaid with gold, of which some twenty examples have been found in historical Hungary.[8] These objects served to decorate small leather satchels in which the early Hungarians kept their fire-making implements. The delicately worked covers were obviously a mark of the bearer's rank, since they have only been found in graves of high-ranking persons. Only one such cover has come to light so far outside Hungary (in Semionovo in Russia, in an area occupied by the Tsheremiss),[9] so that we are dealing here with a unique Hungarian artistic development, of which the sole 'foreign' example may well have originated from Hungarian territory.

The gold and silverwork in question is of such great variety and manifests the outlook and cultural concepts of the early Hungarians in so many ways, that it cannot possibly be ascribed to a single workshop or to a small group of Persian silversmiths working for the Hungarians. It is not only that the large number of the finds negatives any such suggestions: the general character of all these objects shows such a basic unity of style and spiritual outlook and the technique with which they have been executed is so self-assured and masterly, that we must regard them as products of an indigenous Hungarian culture, preceded by centuries of development.[10]

Furthermore, application of Persian ornamental forms and motifs is not limited to early Hungarian metalwork. We find the *palmette* and similar motifs time and time again on carved bone-plates decorating wooden articles, such as bows, quivers and saddles.[11] Indeed, Persian motifs must have also become traditional features of Hungarian houses and other buildings constructed of timber in the pre-Christian era, for the *palmette* keeps recurring in the stonework of the early Christian churches in Hungary as one of the favourite motifs used by the masons. In the absence of any western counterparts, we must conclude that this was a case of transfer of an established decorative procedure from one architectural medium to another.[12]

We are thus faced with a thriving Hungarian art, completely moulded to the needs and mentality of the Magyar conquerors, yet expressing itself in the standard forms of the Sassanian period of the Persian Empire (224 to 651 A.D.) The fact that this Hungarian-Sassanian art makes its appearance three centuries after the end of the reign of the Sassanides in Persia, suggests that it must have been adopted by the Hungarians at least three hundred years prior to their arrival in their present homeland and maintained by them in a basically unaltered form through their long journey in time and space.

This fundamental conservatism of tenth century Hungarian art and the fact that in spite of its Sassanian formal expression it had a strong Hungarian character, further suggest that the early Hungarians did not simply copy the Persian forms but grew up with them as these forms were being developed. In other words, the Magyars must have been in intimate contact with Sassanian Persia from the third to the sixth centuries, so as to make the art of the latter their own and to take it with them as a living entity when they departed from the scene.

Another feature of early Hungarian culture indicative of Persian and Near Eastern influences is the prevalence of the lion as a heraldic animal. The coat of arms of the first Hungarian royal house, the House of Arpád, contained seven lions and there is a lion carved in the crystal sphere constituting the head of the Hungarian coronation sceptre, dating from about 950. The lion also appears as a symbol of sovereignty on a painting in the royal chapel of Béla III (1173-1196) in Esztergom. This painting depicts a highly stylised lion in a pose which is characteristic of the representation of the lion in Near Eastern heraldry.[13] The Near Eastern origin of the Esztergom lion is reinforced by the use of the tree of life and other symbols which two writers, working quite independently of one another, have recently traced back to ancient Mesopotamia.[14]

It is quite clear then that the lions in the Hungarian royal coat of arms were not adopted from the West after the conversion of the Magyars to Christianity, especially as the lion makes its first appearance in Western European heraldry in 1164,[15] more than two hundred years after the making of the Hungarian royal sceptre. Furthermore, the lion also figures prominently in the coats of arms of high-ranking Hungarian clans and families of the Conquest period, such as the Elöd (Csák), Ond (Bor-Kalán), Tuhutum (Zsombor), Gyula (Kán) and Ajtony clans. Of these, the lion in the Gyula shield also stands in a typical Near Eastern pose.[16]

The Magyars of the Conquest period therefore must have brought the lion with them as a heraldic animal and since the only place where they could have become acquainted with it was the Near East, it is reasonable to assume that they lived in that area for an extended period. This means that they must have been at least as far south as the neighbourhood of Persia, although the Esztergom lion with its Mesopotamian characterisation and symbolism strongly suggests that they resided at one time even further to the south, in the region of the Tigris and the Euphrates (see Chapter 7).

It is also interesting to note that in depicting a legendary fight between Saint Ladislas, the most popular mediaeval king of Hungary (1077-1095), and a Cuman warrior, Hungarian artists of the Middle Ages invariably show the king dressed in pure white, with a white horse, whereas the Cuman wears black or dark clothes. This clearly symbolises the cosmic struggle between light and darkness which is the basic concept of Persian religion and indicates that traces of that religion were surviving among Hungarians even after their conversion to Christianity.[17]

Recent investigations of mediaeval Hungarian personal and place names indicate that the Hungarians of the Conquest period were accompanied by a sizeable Iranian minority which settled in the south-western corner of the country, the subsequent counties of Vas and Zala, and took a substantial part in the early western campaigns of the Magyars. These Iranians, called *káliz*, were in charge of the iron foundries of Western Hungary, essential for manufacturing weapons, and also had a military responsibility as frontier guards. They were Mohammedans which led to their enforced dispersal all over Hungary in the Christian era.[18] Whilst more research will have to be done on this subject before we can form any definite conclusions, the metalworking abilities of these Iranians suggest that they were Persians proper who probably joined the Hungarians after the adoption of Islam in Persia in the seventh century. It is clear of course, that the main body of the Magyars was no longer occupying a territory directly adjoining Persia at that time, but they may well have acquired this Persian element through the mediation of the Hungarians who remained south of the Caucasus.

We also cannot exclude the possibility that these Persians went north with the Hungarians when the two nations parted company and were converted to Mohammedanism when their own people adopted that religion. In either event, the existence of a Persian minority within the Hungarian ethnic body suggests extended direct contact leading to the absorption of Persian elements.

When all these Persian connections of the early Hungarians are taken into account, they add up to a powerful argument that the Magyars must have lived in the immediate neighbourhood of Persia over a long period. The predominance of Sassanian art forms and symbols indicates that this period coincided, at least partly, with the amalgamation between the proto-Magyars and the Huns of the Caucasus. This is confirmed by the fact that the Persian Empire began to be active in the Caucasian region in the third century A.D., pressing hard on the Armenians and repeatedly invoking assistance of the Huns. The Hun-Magyar-Persian relationship therefore must have alternated between peaceful coexistence and mutual warfare, until the pressure from the south, aggravated by Byzantine interference, became too much for the Huns and Magyars and they departed for the north.

We have so far established that a branch of the Huns played an important part in the formation of the Hungarians and that this process took place in the southern Caucasus between the second century B.C. and the fourth century A.D. It now remains to be seen which people or peoples furnished the remainder of the ethnic material from which the early Hungarians were formed.

CHAPTER 7

The Sumerians

The Sumerians settled in Mesopotamia around 3500 B.C. and remained the dominant race there until about 1800 B.C., when the Amorites — better known as Babylonians — put an end to them as a political, ethnic and linguistic entity.[1] Between these two dates, they created the first high civilisation of mankind and their impact on the cultures of the surrounding nations was felt for many centuries after their eventual disappearance. Their language remained in cultic and diplomatic use in the Near East until the middle of the first millenium B.C., whilst their cuneiform system of writing was successively adopted by the Akkadians, Assyrians, Babylonians, Hurrians, Hittites, Canaanites, Persians, Elamites and Urartians, and certain varieties of late Babylonian and Assyrian survived as written languages in cuneiform almost down to the time of Christ. Sumerian deities and religious concepts found similarly wide acceptance and their technological achievements, ranging from the invention of the wheel to a highly artistic use of metals, had even more far-reaching effects. Our twentieth century civilisation, with its Graeco-Roman and Semitic background, ultimately goes back to Sumerian foundations, so that directly or indirectly, all mankind is in the debt of the innovating spirit of the Sumerians.

The main settlements of the Sumerians were in Lower Mesopotamia where they founded city-states vying with each other for hegemony. Ur, Uruk, Kish, Nippur, Lagash and Eridu were their main centres of power and wealth, although smaller towns are also known. They called this area *Ki-engi*, the land of Engi. There were also Sumerians in Upper Mesopotamia before the arrival of the Semitic Akkadians and this part of the country was called *Ki-uri*.[2] The designations Sumer and Sumerian were not known to the Sumerians themselves: these names are Semitic corruptions.[3] It is perhaps sad and ironical that these talented people should be remembered by a name given to them by vassal tribes which ultimately brought about their downfall but then, the fact is that they left behind no name for themselves as an ethnic entity, only political and geographical designations.

The Sumerians were so well and truly buried by the dust and rubble of history, that their very existence remained hidden until the middle of the last century, when study of cuneiform records revealed an ancient, non-Semitic language. The first discoverers, Rawlinson and Oppert, called this language 'Scythian' and recognised the people speaking it as the inventor of cuneiform writing. Oppert subsequently sought to establish a relationship between this language and Hungarian, Turkish and Mongolian, and expressed the view that it was closest to the Ugro-Finnish linguistic group. Later, in a lecture delivered before the ethnographic and historical section of the French Society of Numismatics and Archaeology in 1869, he was the first to identify this language as 'Sumerian' and in the same breath he declared, supporting his contention with lexical and grammatical analogies, that it had close affinities with Turkish, Finnish and Hungarian. Another leading early Sumerologist, Lenormant, stated his conviction that this ancient language stood nearest to the Ugro-Finnish branch of the 'Turanian' group and that within this branch, it bore closer resemblance to the Ugric than the Finnish languages.[4] For the first twenty years after the discovery of Sumerian, these views dominated the scientific world until they became obscured by an absurd theory proposed by Halevy.

Halevy, who had made his way from Bucharest to Paris and there became the leading authority on Semitology, put forward the theory in 1874 that Sumerian was the artificial language of Semitic priests and that no such people ever existed. He defended his views with great vehemence, swaying at times even such great savants as Delitzsch, and due to his tenacity which did not waver even in extreme old age, he managed to cloud the issue until his death in 1917. Indeed, the confusion he created in linguistic circles was so profound that up to the present day, no well-known Sumerologist has been prepared to make a definitive statement as to the precise linguistic classification of Sumerian beyond stating that it is an agglutinative language.[5]

The notion of a language 'without any known relative', as some savants still maintain Sumerian was, is of course highly suspect, as it presupposes either that such language had developed in a complete vacuum or that all its relatives have mysteriously disappeared. The first of these alternatives is clearly an impossibility. There is no linguistic vacuum on this earth, not even in the Pacific islands or on the most inaccessible mountains. As to the second, it is extremely unlikely that such a highly talented and versatile people as the Sumerians could have evolved without developing linguistic relationships with a large number of peoples. Can one really suppose that all such peoples are now extinct? It is more reasonable to assume that those who are unable to find any relatives for the Sumerians are simply not looking hard enough.

Indeed, whilst the controversy raged in the West whether Sumerian was a genuine language at all, a slender but steady stream of opinion was building up in Hungary, asserting the relationship between Sumerian and Ural-Altaic languages, and in patricular, Hungarian. The first Hungarian writer to propound this theory was Sándor Giesswein who in his two-volume work, *Mizraim és Asszur* (Budapest, 1887) compared the relationship between Sumerian on the one hand and Finno-Ugrian and Turco-Tartar languages on the other to that between Sanskrit and modern Indo-Germanic languages, and stated expressly that Sumerian was related to Hungarian.

A few years later Zsófia Torma, the noted archaeologist, published the results of her excavations in Transylvania, *Ethnographische Analogien* (Jena, 1894), in which she discerned close similarity between the pottery and other material brought to light by her and ancient Babylonian finds, and declared that the Magyars brought with them the culture of the Sumerians and also absorbed many Sumerian elements in their language.

In 1897, Gyula Ferenczy published a short book on the Sumerians, *Szumer és Akkád* (Debrecen, 1897), asserting that they were an 'ancient Turanian people' and that their language was closely related to Hungarian. In the ensuing years, the highly regarded Hungarian periodical *Ethnografia* printed successive articles by Géza Nagy, Ede Mahler and János Galgóczy, all dealing with the relationship between Sumerian and Hungarian and stressing that Sumerian language and culture had a strong bearing on the question of the ethnic origin of the Magyars. Galgóczy was particularly active in this field and in addition to contributing numerous articles to *Ethnografia,* he also wrote in the Hungarian journals *Századok, Keleti Szemle* and *Magyar Nyelvör,* and between 1909 and 1914, was also a frequent contributor to the *Zeitschrift für Assyrologie.*[6]

It must be emphasised that the writers above referred to were all reputable Hungarian historians and linguists who put forward their arguments on an academic level and, in the case of articles, in scientific periodicals of the highest standing. The first Hungarian Sumerologist to appeal to public opinion was Ede Somogyi who, having achieved some distinction as an encyclopaedist by editing the *Magyar Lexikon* from 1878 onward, became a sub-editor of the well-known Hungarian daily, *Budapesti Hirlap,* in 1889 and thereafter wrote several articles in his paper on the question of Sumerian-Hungarian relationship. In 1903, he published a book entitled *Szumirok és magyarok,* in which he sought to demonstrate with grammatical examples and a detailed dictionary that Sumerian was an Ural-Altaic language and stood nearest to Hungarian.[7] This created a great stir and the Hungarian Academy of Sciences felt obliged to refer it to Bernát Munkácsi, a distinguished linguist of the Finno-Ugrian school, for an opinion. Munkácsi put in an adverse report, as a result of which the Academy rejected Somogyi's book as a 'dilettante work' — which it may well have been — and declared that 'the special emphasis placed on the importance of Sumerian cuneiform writings from the point of view of Hungarian prehistory is based on error and cannot be justified with scientific credibility'.[8]

Galgóczy immediately attacked Munkácsi's findings and this is when a remarkable development took place. In an article defending his report, Munkácsi conceded that Sumerian and Ural-Altaic languages had a certain common vocabulary and proceeded to give a number of examples from the fields of domestic life, nature, cultural concepts and social relations. He declared, however, that these were 'very ancient loanwords', acquired

71

through the mediation of other languages. In his opinion, there were too many grammatical differences between Sumerian and Hungarian to permit the assumption of any closer relationship.[9]

Having made an important concession, Munkácsi did not resile from it in his later writings and indeed, he repeatedly referred to the Sumerian connection in placing the ancestral home of Hungarians and other Finno-Ugrian peoples in the northern Caucasus[10] and in tracing Assyrian loanwords in the Hungarian language.[11] The Hungarian Academy, however, maintained its previous commitment to the Finno-Ugrian ethnic theory (see Chapter 3) and Munkácsi's *rapprochement* to the Sumerists was largely ignored.

Notwithstanding official rejection of the suggested Sumerian-Hungarian relationship, the question continued to occupy the minds of some Hungarian linguists and historians and, in addition to linguistic studies, an effort was also made to invoke the aid of comparative anthropology. In his work *Babylonia és Assyria* (Budapest, 1906), Ede Mahler analysed Sumerian racial types as appearing on Sumerian bas-reliefs and statuary, and concluded that they stood nearest to the Turanian race and were to be considered as one of the branches of the oldest predecessors of Turkic peoples. Unfortunately, as the study of prehistory in Hungary was entirely dominated by the linguists at that time, these anthropological comparisons were not pursued.

After World War I, the Sumerian question well-nigh disappeared from public discussion in Hungary until Zsigmond Varga, Professor of Oriental Languages at the famous Calvinist theological college of Debrecen, published a monumental work in 1942, entitled *Ötezer év távolából,* in which he demonstrated with a detailed analysis of Sumerian grammar and vocabulary that Sumerian was related to Hungarian and Finno-Ugrian and Turco-Tartar languages and was an independent branch of the Ural-Altaic family of languages. In addition to linguistic comparisons, he also relied on religious concepts, funerary rites and popular beliefs and superstitions to show an affinity between Sumerians and the present Ural-Altaic peoples.

Owing to the tragic events which followed in Hungary soon after the publication of Varga's work, his findings did not receive the attention they deserved but the seed had been sown and when the successive waves of the Great Hungarian Diaspora settled down in various parts of the world, a surprisingly virile and widespread Sumerist school began to arise, cultivated by Hungarian refugee linguists and historians.

In 1951, Ida Bobula published her *Sumerian Affiliations* in Washington, in which she identified a large number of basic Hungarian words as of Sumerian derivation and also found similarities between Hungarian and Akkadian words of everyday use. She also analysed affinities between Hungarian and Sumerian religious concepts, mythology, funerary habits and astrological notions, and concluded that these linguistic and cultural affiliations were due to the influence of a group of learned Sumerians who took refuge among the ancestors of the Hungarians after the collapse of Sumerian rule in Mesopotamia. In a subsequent work published ten years later, Bobula also demonstrated that a large number of Hungarian words hitherto considered as Slavonic loanwords, were of Sumerian or Akkadian origin.[12] She wrote numerous articles on the Sumerian-Hungarian relationship and ultimately formed the conclusion that Hungarians were direct descendants of the Sumerians, although she conceded that a great deal of research still had to be done on this question.[13]

Bobula's work strongly influenced a number of Hungarian historians abroad, of whom the most outstanding was the late Viktor Padányi in Australia. In his *Dentumagyaria* (Buenos Aires, 1963), Padányi made an attempt at re-writing Hungarian prehistory on the basis of the Mesopotamian origin of the Magyars or at least a substantial part of them, and although many of his propositions still lack positive proof — we hasten to add, unavoidably so — his work created great interest even in Hungary itself. Another Hungarian historian, Sándor Nagy, in America, analysed Hungarian personal and place names occurring in early mediaeval records and, considering these to be of Sumerian origin, concluded that a substantial part of the Hungarian ethnic body must have been formed by successive waves of Sumerian settlers in the Carpathian basin.[14]

In the strictly linguistic field, Sándor Csöke in Austria carried out painstaking research in the late sixties,[15] proclaiming the direct descent of the Hungarian language from Sumerian. More recently, András Zakar of Budapest, using the methods of glottochronology, has shown that of one hundred basic words in Hungarian, compiled in accordance with Professor Hymes' word list, fifty-five were of Sumerian and nine of Akkadian derivation.[16]

Another leading Hungarian protagonist of Sumerian-Hungarian linguistic and ethnic identity is Ferenc Badiny Jós, Professor of Sumerology at the Jesuit University of Buenos Aires, who has written several works on this topic and has recently strongly defended his propositions at the twenty-ninth International Congress of Orientalists in Paris.[17]

The views initially expressed by Rawlinson, Oppert and Lenormant have therefore been reinforced by Hungarian research extending over a century. It is worth noting that the distinguished Finnish Assyriologist, Harri Holma, also held the view that Sumerian and Finno-Ugrian languages were related, although most of his work in this field was never published.[18] The question remains now whether the available evidence indicates a direct descent of Hungarians, at least partly, from the Sumerians or we are merely faced with a linguistic relationship between Sumerian and Hungarian in much the same way as Hungarian is related to other Ural-Altaic languages? As a third alternative, the possibility of extensive borrowing by Hungarian from Sumerian also must be considered.

Since these questions cannot be answered without determining the nature of the linguistic affinity between Sumerian and Hungarian, let us see briefly how much can be safely accepted from the assertions made by various writers on this subject.

As a result of researches by Bobula, Csöke and Zakar, we have fairly extensive comparative tables of Sumerian and Hungarian vocabularies of which the following examples indicate the degree of existing relationship:

Sumerian	*Hungarian*
ur (lord)	*ur* (lord)
nin (lady)	*néni* (elder woman)

Sumerian	Hungarian
nab (sun)	*nap* (sun)
hud (light)	*hold*, archaic and provincial *hód*, *hud* (moon)
Isten (the One, God)	*Isten* (God)
lil (soul)	*lélek*, arch. *lilk* (soul)
ul (womb, lap)	*öl* (lap)
kus (skin, body)	*hus* (flesh)
bur (blood)	*vér* (blood)
gis (hand)	*kéz* (hand)
ussa (younger brother)	*öccs* (younger brother)
ari (daughter-in-law)	*ara* (bride)
us (begets)	*ös* (ancestor)
kurun (bread)	*kenyér*, arch. *kerenye* (bread)
edin (barrel)	*edény*, arch. *edin* (vessel)
dal (vessel)	*tál* (plate)
duk (vessel)	*tok* (sheath); *tök* (gourd)
sabur (vessel)	*csupor*, prov. *szapor* (small vessel)
dar (food offering for the dead)	*tor* (funerary meal)
izi (fire)	*izzik* (glows)
bil (burns)	*föl* (cooks)
sil (cuts)	*szel* (slices)
sab (cuts)	*szab* (cuts)
hun (rests)	*huny* (sleeps, rests)
tar (severs, cuts)	*tör* (breaks)
sir (cries)	*sir* (cries)
li (cries)	*ri* (cries)
bur (makes a hole)	*fur* (bores)
bul (blows)	*fuj, ful* (blows)
ru (carves, engraves)	*ró* (carves, engraves)
mas (twin, like)	*más* (copy, like)
gur (container of cereals)	*góré* (corn shed)
dan, tan (explains, clarifies)	*tan-it* (teaches); *tan-ács* (counsel, council)

Sumerian	Hungarian
til (inhabits, sits)	*tel-ep* (settlement)
	tel-ek (block of land)
dingir (god)	*tenger* (immense, sea);
	tündér (fairy)
itu (month)	*idö* (time)
ab (water)	*hab* (wave, foam)
al (sound)	*hall* (hears)
rig (speaks)	*rege* (saga);
	regé-l (recites)
sa (network)	*szö* (weaves)
retu (meadow)	*rét* (meadow)
kabbar (fat)	*kövér* (fat)
gada (fringed loincloth)	*gatya*, prov. *gagya* (fringed loincloth)
gar (makes, manufactures)	*gyárt* (manufactures)
gur (bends, is bent)	*görbe* (bent)
guz (centre)	*góc* (centre)
gam (bends)	*gamó* (shepherd'crook, bent stick)
dule (over, more than)	*tul* (over, more than)
dib (walks)	*tip-eg* (walks daintily)
dug (swells)	*dag-ad* (swells)
	dag-anat (swelling)
eri (goes)	*ere-d* (goes, starts)
es (evening)	*est* (evening)
zid (is angry)	*szid* (scolds)
has (splits)	*has-it* (splits)
izi (hastens)	*izi-be* (in haste)
indi (course)	*ind-it* (sets off)
	ind-ul (starts)
kid (binds)	*köt* (binds)
kur (circle)	*kör* (circle)
nad (great)	*nagy* (great)
nam (no)	*nem* (no)
pa (tree)	*fa* (tree)
pa (head)	*fö, fej* (head)
bur (ear)	*fül* (ear)

Sumerian	Hungarian
sa (mouth)	*száj* (mouth)
hal (dies)	*hal* (dies)
gil (murders)	*gyil-kol* (murders)
	gyil-ok (murder weapon)
ud (road)	*ut* (road)
me (we)	*mi* (we)
sur (stabs)	*szur* (stabs)

These examples will suffice to show that whilst in some instances there is remarkable correspondence between Sumerian and Hungarian vocabularies both as to form and meaning, in other cases the similarity is no closer than what exists between Sumerian and Ural-Ultaic languages in general. Indeed, it is clear from the comparative analyses of Sumerian words published by Csöke and Zakar that where the relationship with Hungarian is of this remoter kind, there are usually equally close, and sometimes closer, correspondences in Finno-Ugrian or Turco-Tartar languages.

It is also significant that there are a number of basic Hungarian words — such as *kéz* (hand), *vér* (blood), *kö* (stone), *szarv* (horn), *szem* (eye), to name only a few — which have much closer equivalents in Finnish, Estonian and related languages, than in Sumerian. A certain degree of relationship with Sumerian can be demonstrated also as regards words in this category but it is of a more distant nature. These aspects of Sumerian and Hungarian vocabularies strongly suggest that there were two phases of intensive contact between the peoples speaking these languages: one in the very distant past when they were also in close proximity to other Ural-Altaic peoples and a second one much later, during the Sumerian era in Mesopotamia, when the proto-Hungarians acquired those Sumerian words which are still contained in virtually unaltered form and meaning in their language. For some time in the interval between these two phases, the proto-Hungarians remained in the general area occupied by Finno-Ugrian peoples and certain further similarities between their respective languages developed.

This supposition of a second contact between the proto-Magyars and the Sumerians is confirmed by the very clear adoption of the Sumerian numeral *vun* (ten) in Hungarian. The Hungarian word for 'ten' is *tiz*, yet 'forty', 'fifty', 'sixty', 'seventy', 'eighty' and 'ninety' are respectively *negy-ven* (four 'ven'), *öt-ven* (five 'ven'), *hat-van* (six 'van'), *het-ven* (seven 'ven'), *nyolc-van* (eight 'van') and *kilenc-ven* (nine 'ven'). 'Ven' and 'van', varying for vocalic harmony, have no meaning whatever in Hungarian,[19] nor have they any relationship to any known Hungarian suffix, so that the conclusion that they are derived from the Sumerian *vun* is virtually inescapable. This being so, it seems very likely that the composite numerals referred to were formed in Hungarian when the proto-Magyars were familiar with the Sumerian word for 'ten' and probably used it themselves in everyday dealings. As no similar correspondence can be observed in other Ural-Altaic languages, this point of contact must be placed in the Sumerian period in Mesopotamia.

Further proof of close Hungarian-Sumerian contacts in Mesopotamia is furnished by the use of the word *ur* in both languages. In Sumerian, this word has several meanings (man, guard, lord), whereas in Hungarian it only means 'lord'. In the last-mentioned sense, it appears to have been a royal title in Sumer at various times, as it occurs in the names of several Sumerian kings, such as Ur-Nammu, Ur-Nanshe, Ur-Zababa. Now, it is significant that in early Hungarian, the title *ur* was reserved for members of the royal family and other high-ranking Hungarians. The proto-Magyars therefore must have adopted this word with one specific meaning, namely 'lord', and for one specific purpose, to designate their royalty, and it is quite obvious that this borrowing must have taken place whilst the Sumerians were so using the word *ur* in Mesopotamia. The total absence of this word from other Ural-Altaic languages confirms this point.

Turning now to Sumerian grammar, we find a similar dichotomy in its relationship to Hungarian as in the field of vocabulary. Sumerian is an agglutinative language with numerous suffixes and no grammatical gender and also has many other features in common with Ural-Altaic languages. These were analysed in great detail by Zsigmond Varga who demonstrated quite convincingly that Sumerian was an Ural-Altaic language.

Varga, however, never claimed that the grammatical structure of Sumerian was more closely related to Hungarian than other Ural-Altaic languages and indeed, in various aspects of Sumerian grammar he found better correspondences in other Ural-Altaic languages than in Hungarian. As far as the writer is aware, Varga's work still stands unparalleled in Sumerian-Hungarian comparative philology and his general findings have not been superseded. Consequently, it seems that as far as the general grammatical structure of Sumerian is concerned, it only bears such basic relationship to Hungarian as it does to other Ural-Altaic languages.

On the other hand, there are some specific features of Sumerian grammar which show a remarkable correspondence with Hungarian. This is particularly so in the case of certain suffixes. For example, the Sumerian suffix *sag* (-hood, -ship) corresponds exactly with the Hungarian suffix *ság, ség* (again varying for vocalic harmony), not only in form but also in meaning. Thus the Sumerian *ursag* (lordship) is *uraság* (lordship) in Hungarian. Although the Hungarian *s* is pronounced like *sh* in English, the original Sumerian pronunciation has been preserved in some Hungarian words such as *ország* (realm, country), which incidentally is also derived from the Sumerian *ursag* as its mediaeval form was still *urusag*.

Again, the Sumerian verb *ag* (makes, does) which is also used as a suffix in Sumerian, is clearly reflected in the Hungarian suffix *og* (occasionally *eg* for vocalic harmony), for example *kavar-og* (is stirred up, is turbulent; *kavar* = stirs), *fintor-og* (makes a face; *fintor* = a facial distortion). This is particularly obvious in the case of onomatopoeic (sound-imitating) verbs in Hungarian, such as *sáp-og* (quacks), *szip-og* (sniffles), *szisz-eg* (hisses), *csip-og* (chirps), *dad-og* (stutters). In all such cases, the first syllable imitates the sound made and the suffix *og* signifies the making of such sound.

We are therefore again faced with the phenomenon that whereas Sumerian grammar as a whole only bears a basic resemblance to Hungarian, certain specific features of it occur in modern Hungarian in identical form. This confirms our previous suggestion that after very ancient initial contacts, followed by a long period of separation, Sumerians and proto-Hungarians again lived side by side for a considerable time in Mesopotamia during which period certain aspects of Sumerian grammar found their way into Hungarian.

This Mesopotamian coexistence is strongly supported by the occurrence of Akkadian words in Hungarian. As Akkadian is a Semitic language, there is no possibility whatever that its similarities with Hungarian vocabulary developed in some distant ancestral homeland. The Hungarians must have acquired these Akkadian words in Mesopotamia and no other place. In a sense, therefore, the presence of Akkadian loanwords in Hungarian, attested by the researches of Munkácsi, Varga, Bobula, Csöke and Zakar, is even more important for the study of Hungarian prehistory than similarities between Sumerian and Hungarian. Here are a few examples:

Akkadian	*Hungarian*
kasaru (binds)	*koszoru* (wreath)
salatu (cuts, slices)	*szeletel* (slices)
dalilu (sings)	*dalol* (sings)
mussulu (copy)	*másol* (copies)
gimilu (spares)	*kimél* (spares)
ruggumu (complain in law)	*rágalom* (libel)
kasadu (sleeps)	*kushad* (lies low)
tallu (vessel)	*tál* (dish)
liku (opening)	*lyuk*, prov. *lik* (hole, opening)
kalappatu (hammer)	*kalapács* (hammer)

There is therefore strong linguistic evidence that the ancestors of Hungarians lived in the Mesopotamian region during the third millenium B.C. and possibly even earlier. This evidence is supported by definite traces of Sumerian mythology and religious concepts in Hungarian folklore. The cult of the Great Stag, one of the personifications of the Sumerian god Enki, is reflected in numerous Hungarian Christmas and New Year's Eve *regös* chants.[20] It is perhaps not without significance that the melodies of these chants differ markedly from the pentatonic folk-songs prevalent in old Hungarian music and are generally regarded as of much more ancient origin.[21] Although the cult of a benevolent stag divinity is common to many peoples, Hungarians have also preserved his name, *Dara-mah* (Hungarian *Doromó, Durumó*), and the memory of his son *Dumuzig* (later Tammuz) survived in the Hungarian pagan god *Damachek.*[22]

The early Hungarians also had a benevolent fertility goddess called *Boldogasszony* (Blessed Lady) who has left many traces in Hungarian folklore and ultimately became identified with the Virgin Mary. This goddess is strongly reminiscent of the Sumerian Bau who, like her, was the protector of plants and the harvest and also of women in childbirth. It cannot be a mere coincidence that traditional Hungarian harvest-festivals are held on the feast of the Assumption (in Hungarian called *Nagyboldogasszony*, 'great Boldogasszony') in much the same way as the Sumerians held a special feast in honour of Bau when they first ate the new bread. Again, the Hungarian custom called *Boldogasszony pohara* (cup of the Boldogasszony), the offering of a cup of wine to the Boldogasszony by a woman after her childbirth, can be seen on Sumerian cylinder seals depicting women approaching the goddess Bau and offering her a drinking vessel.[23] It is also important to note that several feastdays of Mary in Hungary have names with clear agricultural connotation — such as *Gyümölcsoltó Boldogasszony* ('fruit-grafting Boldogasszony', 25 March), *Sarlós Boldogasszony* ('Boldogasszony of the sickle', 2 July) — which have no bearing whatever on their Christian religious significance and can only be explained with the survival of pagan traditions. All these matters point strongly to the cult of the Sumerian goddess Bau.

Again, the Hungarian funerary habit of taking the body to the grave on a cart drawn by six white oxen corresponds with finds in the royal graves of Ur.[24]

Turning now to an entirely different aspect of Sumerian-Hungarian relations, all three native Hungarian breeds of dogs — the *puli*, the *kuvasz* and the *komondor* — can be traced back to ancient Mesopotamia and even their names have Sumerian etymologies.[25]

Absorption of linguistic and cultural elements to such a high degree and acquisition of all three indigenous Hungarian dog breeds are unlikely to have taken place without some intermingling and intermarriage between the proto-Magyars and the Sumerians. The density of the populations of the Sumerian city-states — estimated at half a million each for Ur, Kish, Nippur, Eridu and Lagash[26] — and the overflow of Sumerian cultural influence, and at times political hegemony, into all the areas surrounding Mesopotamia proper since at least 3000 B.C.,[27] make such a process extremely probable. It is therefore reasonable to assume that the Sumerians contributed to the ethnic formation of the Hungarians during the third millenium B.C. to a fairly significant degree. On the other hand, because of certain fundamental differences between Sumerian and Hungarian grammar and also by reason of appreciable divergences between Sumerian and Hungarian vocabularies, a direct descent of Hungarians from Sumerians cannot be supposed. It appears therefore that the basic material which underwent an infusion of Sumerian blood, the proto-Magyar people, was of a different stock, although the two may have been related in a distant way.

As regards the geographical area occupied by the proto-Magyars during the Sumerian period, it could not have been south, west or north-west of Sumer, for these areas were inhabited by Semites. It must have been therefore east or north-east of Sumerian territory. Since the presence of Akkadian loanwords in Hungarian postulates a region where regular contact with the Akkadians was possible, whilst enabling the even more intimate relations with the Sumerians to be maintained, the most likely place for the Hungarian homeland during this period is the hill country between the Tigris and the Zagros mountains, part of the ancient land of Subartu. This country was under strong Sumerian influence during the whole of the third millenium B.C. and if the Hungarians in fact lived there during that period, the Sumerian elements shown by their language and culture can be easily explained.

It now remains to be seen whether we can fit the Hungarians into Subartu and if so, how they got up to Transcaucasia.

CHAPTER 8

Subartu and the Hurri People

From the earliest times in Sumer, we find in written records people described as *Subir, Shubur* or simply *Su,* living peacefully among the Sumerians and later on also the Akkadians, sometimes as slaves but also as free men following various occupations, such as bakers, smiths, scribes and even chief scribes. The country where these people emanated from was called in Sumerian *Subir-ki* (Subir land) and in Akkadian *Subartu* which has become its accepted designation among historians.[1]

The precise geographical area occupied by Subartu is somewhat uncertain and it may well have varied during various periods of Sumerian history. It is clear, however, that the name signified a country rather than a people. During the Old Akkadian period, it appears that this country comprised the territory between the Tigris and the mountains in the east, as well as that part of northern Mesopotamia which later became Assyria.[2] This is a vast area and it seems extremely unlikely that the people inhabiting it all belonged to the same ethnic element.

Sumerian and Akkadian sources dating back to c. 2300 B.C., reveal the existence in Subartu of a clearly identifiable people which seven centuries later appears under the name of Hurrians. The frequent occurrence of personal and place names of Hurrian derivation all over Subartu led some historians to conclude that Hurrians and the original inhabitants of Subartu were one and the same people.[3] However, Ignace Gelb has demonstrated by careful analysis of early records and the names of people described in them as Subarians that they and the Hurrians belonged to two different ethnic units, with the Hurrians being comparative newcomers in areas previously occupied by the Subarians.[4] Indeed, the independent arrival of the Hurrians in these areas is attested by archaeological finds suggesting steady infiltration of a people bearing their characteristics from the early part of the third millenium onwards.⁵ On the other hand, the Subarians appear to have been there long before the settlement of the Sumerians in Mesopotamia.⁶

There is therefore evidence of two distinct ethnic elements in Subartu during the third millenium B.C. and there may well have been more. No one has yet investigated the ethnic origins of the Subarians proper⁷ but it seems clear that they were neither Semites nor Indo-Aryans. This leaves us with the third major ethnic group in that area, the Turanian or Ural-Altaic peoples, and it is a fair conclusion that the Subarians belonged to them. The very fact that the Sumerians and, as we shall see, the Hurrians also belonged to this group, confirms the existence of a vast conglomerate of Turanian peoples in and around Mesopotamia in this period. This being so, there is no difficulty at all in making the assumption, already foreshadowed in Chapter 7, that the early Hungarians inhabited Subartu in ancient times.

The connections of the early Magyars with Subartu are also supported by their ancient name of *Sabartoi asphaloi,* recorded by Constantinus Porphyrogenetus (Chapter 2).⁸

Although the Subarians and, initially at least, also the Hurrians living in Sumerian and Akkadian territory, were peaceful enough — probably because they had no alternative — their brethren in Subartu could hardly have been less so. During the Old Akkadian and Ur III periods, i.e., in the latter part of the third millenium B.C., there are several references in Mesopotamian records to repeated warfare between Akkadian and Sumerian rulers and the kings of Subartu. These sources indicate that the Subarian side was represented by a coalition of kings, some of whom had Hurrian names.⁹ The Hurrians therefore must have achieved a position of pre-eminence among the Subarians by that time. This multiplicity of kings also suggests that towards the end of the third millenium B.C., Subartu consisted of several different political units¹⁰ and this is again consistent with its population comprising a number of separate ethnic groups. On the other hand, the ease with which these separate units combined to wage war against the Sumerians and Akkadians indicates that they were culturally closely related and probably belonged to the same basic ethnic stock.

In these wars, the Subarians certainly proved themselves equal to the Sumerians and Akkadians and although they suffered defeat at various times, it was they who, in alliance with the Elamites, brought the third dynasty of Ur to an end around 2029.[11] This was an event of cataclysmic proportions, resulting in a ferocious sacking of Ur and widespread devastation all over Sumer and Akkad[12] which would not have been possible without great mobility on the part of the perpetrators. This postulates use of the horse and it is indeed clear that the Subarians must have been great horsemen, for the very use of that animal reached Mesopotamia from their region.[13] This again suggests that the Subarians were of Turanian race.

When Sumer was overrun by the Babylonians, the Subarians continued to maintain their independence and there were frequent wars between them and the Babylonians. They became particularly troublesome during the reign of Hamurabi (1792-1750 B.C.) which probably indicated that pressure was building up within their area. Contemporary records from this period again keep referring to the kings of Subartu,[14] suggesting political, and perhaps ethnic, divisions in that land.

With the death of Hammurabi (1750 B.C.) the political equilibrium in the Near East came to an end. Shamshi-Adad I of Assyria (1813-1781 B.C.) was already dead, leaving a weak successor, and Egypt was passing through a long period of decay after the fall of the twelfth dynasty (c. 1776 B.C.). In the power-vacuum thus created, a great explosion took place. Assyria was blotted out for two centuries, Babylonia was overrun by the Kassites, and Egypt was invaded by the Hyksos. There is darkness all over the Near East for the next two hundred years and we can at best get a blurred picture of the events that must have taken place. When the dust begins to settle around 1600 B.C., we find a strong Hurrian state in Northern Mesopotamia and the surrounding areas, and sizeable, and more importantly, dominant Hurrian colonies in Assyria, Babylonia, Syria, Palestine, Egypt and Anatolia. This sudden expansion of Hurrians over the whole of the Near East suggests that it was they who suddenly changed the power-structure of the entire area and caused the Kassite and Hyksos invasions, probably driving these peoples before them.[15] It now remains to be seen whether they were not also instrumental in shifting the proto-Magyars to Transcaucasia.

Although Hurrians were present in Northern Mesopotamia and the country between the Tigris and the Zagros mountains from the first half of the third millenium B.C., their home territory was in the region of Lake Van in eastern Anatolia and the highland zone between the Upper Euphrates and the Caucasus.[16] Archaeological finds in this area manifest a general uniformity of material culture from the last quarter to the fourth millenium B.C., suggesting ethnic unity and pointing to continuous occupation by the Hurrians from that time onwards.[17]

It was from this region that the Hurrians apparently burst forth to bring the whole of the Near East under their sway and create a powerful Hurrian state in Northern Mesopotamia, Mitanni, with vassal states in the surrounding areas. It is only after this Hurrian expansion that the name 'Hurri', or more exactly *khurri,* makes its first appearance in contemporary sources and this has led Ungnad to suggest that that name does not designate a people but only a political concept, such as 'federation' or 'union'.[18] However, Hrozny has established that there was also a city called Khurri or Khurra mentioned by that name in Assyrian and Babylonian records which was probably identical with modern Urfa (Edessa) and was the centre of the Hurrian empire.[19] This makes it appear more likely that *khurri* was the name of the Hurrian people in their own language and that they applied the same designation to their capital.[20]

The various forms in which the name Hurrian occurs in the records of surrounding peoples — Hittite *khurlili,* Harrian *khurvule,* Egyptian *khor* or *khuru,* Old Testament *khori* — suggest that the actual Hurrian root of that name was *khur* or *khor,* to which each of their neighbours added its own suffix.

That the Hurrians were occasionally able to transfer their name to peoples subject to them, is clear from the fact that the *khori* of the Bible — whose name has been westernized as Horites — were not Hurrians but Semites who previously lived under Hurrian overlodship.[21]

The Hurrians were keen horsemen who introduced new methods of chariot warfare[22] and were buried with their horses when they died.[23] They were also the first people known to have used a composite bow, constructed of several layers of bone and timbers of different kind, which the Egyptians called the 'Hurrian bow'[24] and which appears to have been the prototype of the powerful weapons of a similar construction used by the Huns, Avars and early Hungarians. All this suggests an Ural-Altaic people and, indeed, the Hurrian language is an agglutinative one which Albright and Lambdin have recently characterised as of a Finno-Ugrian type.[25]

Although the main expansion of the Hurrians was towards the south, there is evidence that they also pushed new ethnic elements into Anatolia, causing disorganisation of the Hittite Empire.[26] Hurrian influence among the Hittites was very strong, manifesting itself in virtually every phase of the Hittite civilisation and underlined by the Hurrian names occurring among members of the Hittite royal family and nobility.[27] However, there was also considerable warfare between these two peoples and it is only reasonable to assume that when the Hurrians depleted their ethnic reserves in the north by expanding towards the south, they shifted some other people or peoples in their place to guard their northern and north-eastern frontiers. At the time this step became necessary, i.e., around the eighteenth century B.C., the Subarians were already living in the foothills of the Kurdish mountains and the mountainous regions of northern Mesopotamia[28] and as they were ethnically related to the Hurrians and their way of life was similar, they must have been a logical choice as replacements.

Assuming, therefore, that the proto-Magyars were part of the Subarians, it appears extremely likely that they were moved to Transcaucasia by the Hurrians. It follows that they must have had a Hurrian aristocracy and must have been initially classified as Hurrians themselves. This was a standard method of conquest and integration among Ural-Altaic peoples throughout their long history and there is no reason to suppose that the Hurrians acted otherwise. Such a process would necessarily involve strong identification by the proto-Magyars with their Hurrian rulers, including assumption of their name and some of their basic national traditions.

87

It is then quite likely that when the proto-Magyars moved to Transcaucasia they became known as Khur or Khor, in much the same way as the six Horite tribes in Palestine bore that name. In time, the initial *kh* probably gave way to the softer *g*, resulting in *Gur* or *Gor*. Since the Sevordik Hungarians were still living in the valley of the river Kur in the twelfth century A.D., it is a fair conclusion that both the name of that river and the ancient city of Gori perpetuate the original name of the Hurrian-ruled proto-Magyars. The same probably applies to their subsequent name Makor or Magor. In Sumerian as well as several Finno-Ugrian languages, the word for the inhabited land or country is *ma* and although this word is no longer part of Hungarian vocabulary, it is still found in Vogul and therefore must have been used by the early Magyars. The land of the Khor or Gor people was therefore called Makhor or Magor and a person from that country was called Magori (the suffix *i* means 'of', 'from'), as would be the case even in present-day Hungarian. Indeed, it is significant that whereas Anonymus calls the ancestral home of the Magyars Moger, he calls the people themselves Mogeri (*Mogerii* in the Latin text). This distinction was therefore still observed in the twelfth century but faded subsequently, just as the distinction between Magor and Gor must have disappeared at an earlier stage.

The people called Makor in the writings of Herodotus and Xenophon were therefore the inhabitants of the land so called who by that time identified themselves by the name of their country, and not the earlier name of Khor or Gor from which the name of the country itself was derived. The earlier name, however, was probably preserved by the neighbours of the Magyars as Gor, and in time Ugor, which must have survived in that region long enough to be transferred to a branch of the Caucasian Huns when they arrived there and merged with the Magyars. The name of the city of Ugarit, which had a strong Hurrian upper stratum,[29] suggests that the designation Ugor may have been even more generally applied to Hurrian-dominated communities in the Near East. Whilst this aspect requires more elucidation, the matters already discussed in this chapter and Chapter 5 make it reasonably clear that the name Ugor by which the Hungarians make their appearance in early Byzantine, Slavic and Frankish sources can be directly traced back to the Hurrian Khor through its subsequent forms of Kur and Gori which were deposited, so to speak, as geographical designations at various stages during the stay of the Magyar people in that area and now testify as to its ethnic identity.

Hurrian influence in the Near East declined markedly around 1,300 B.C. when the state of Mitanni was destroyed by Assyria and the Hurrians did not emerge again as an important factor until they reorganised themselves in the Vannic kingdom of Urartu in the ninth century B.C. During the interval, the Magyars must have been left pretty much to themselves and it is fair to assume that they completely absorbed their thin Hurrian upper class in this period. Indeed, they may have indulged in some southern ventures themselves, for they were a warrior people and the vacuum left by the collapse of Hurrian power must have been very tempting for them. Biblical references to 'Gog in the land of Magog' (Ezekiel 38, 1, 2; 39, 1, 2) are strongly suggestive of 'Gor in the land of Magor' and it surely cannot be ignored that both times the country of Magog is mentioned in the Old Testament (Gen. 10, 2; Ezekiel 38, 1, 2; 39, 1, 2), the context places it in the same geographical area where we later encounter the Makors in Herodotus and Xenophon.[30] There is therefore nothing inherently improbable in the suggestion that the military campaigns of the Magyars may have occasionally taken them as far south as Palestine, making them appear as the scourge of God descending suddenly from a faraway northern land.

These southern escapades were probably even encouraged during the rise and expansion of Urartu in the ninth and eighth centuries B.C. Urartu was a federal state comprising several peoples under Hurrian rule[31] and at the height of its power, its hegemony extended to the Transcaucasian area. An Assyrian source dating from about 735 B.C. refers to the land of Guriana as lying next to the Cimmerians and paying tribute to Urartu.[32] This reference is clearly to the Magyars in their Transcaucasian home, not only because Guriana is an obvious Assyrian distortion of Gur or Guri — confirming the transition from Khur to Gur suggested by us above — but also because the Bible expressly refers to the Cimmerians as living next to the land of Magog (Gen. 10, 2).[33] The Magyars therefore were tributaries of the Urartians and probably took part in some of their campaigns but they maintained a measure of independence, and repeated references to revolts by outlying provinces in the annals of Urartu[34] suggest that, being removed from the centre of Urartian power, the Magyars did not give in easily to this late Hurrian domination.

By this time, the Magyars must have well and truly converted their horsemanship from chariotry to horseriding, as the Urartians did themselves.[35] There is ample evidence in the inscriptions and art of the Urartians that they were proud horsemen and cavalry played a leading part in their army.[36] We must make the same assumption concerning the Magyars in this period. The proximity of the Scythians and Cimmerians, fierce horseriding nomads, also must have had a profound effect on them and the geographic features of their mountainous homeland also militated against the use of chariots. By the eighth century B.C., therefore, and probably much earlier, the Magyars must have conducted all their warfare and most of their daily activities on horseback.

With the collapse of Urartu at the beginning of the sixth century B.C. and the eastward thrust of the Armenians at the same time,[37] the Magyars were effectively sealed off from the south and did not again play a role in the Near East until the advent of the Huns in the Caucasus. In the intervening period, they must have lived as an entirely free and independent nation, as the pre-Turkic or 'Ugrian' words in Hungarian relating to state and political affairs — such as *fejedelem* (ruling prince, king), *uralkodó* (ruler), *ur* (lord), *ország* (realm), *birodalom* (empire), *tartomány* (province), *föember* (chief official), *elökelö* (high-ranking), *elöljáró* (magistrate), *országgyülés* (parliament), *nemes* (noble), *had* (army), *hadnagy* (general), *uradalom* (lord's holding), to mention only a few — testify to a high degree of political organisation. When the Hun brothers arrived, therefore, the Magyars received them entirely on equal terms politically and probably had a lot to teach them in other respects.

Since the presence of the Magyars in Transcaucasia in the pre-Christian era is not generally postulated in modern historiography, no archaeological investigations have been directed so far at tracing their occupation of the Kur valley and adjoining areas. A surprising find has come to light, however, in Karmir Blur, near Yerevan in Armenia. Among the ruins of a large Urartian fortress dating from the middle of the seventh century B.C., a carved stone jar with hunting scenes was found which Piotrovskii, the greatest contemporary expert on Urartian art, considers so unusual that he doubts its Urartian origin. The scene carved in relief on the side of the jar, which is now in the Armenian Historical Museum, represents a procession of animals, namely a goat, a lion, a bird sitting on the lion's tail and a stag, followed by an archer resting on one knee, a horseman and a warrior bearing a sword and a shield.[38] Since birds do not normally sit on lion's tails, the entire scene must have a mythical significance. The constellation of bird, stag and archer is strangely reminiscent of one of the hunting scenes on the famous Horn of Lehel, a tenth-century ivory horn found in Hungary, where the archer is in the same position as on the Karmir Blur jar and the bird, again clearly of cultic significance, sits on the stag's back. Since Karmir Blur is very close to what we suggest was ancient Hungarian territory, the recurrence of the same hunting motif seventeen centuries later in Hungary proper cannot be mere coincidence, and the likelihood of direct transmission is strengthened by the cultic character of both finds.

Assuming, therefore, that the carved jar of Karmir Blur was of Hungarian origin, its emergence among the ruins of an Urartian fort furnishes further proof of close Hurrian-Hungarian relations. These can be also traced in another important way. We have already referred to the fact that in early Christian tradition and Moslem mythology Edessa (Urfa) was particularly closely associated with Nimrod (Chapter 1), and we have also pointed out that this city was probably the capital of the Hurrians. It is therefore very likely that Nimrod was a Hurrian mythical figure, or perhaps even an early Hurrian ruler, and that he personifies that people in the Bible and Near Eastern tradition. Biblical references to the role played by him in Assyria are certainly consistent with the Hurrian occupation of that country and although there is no evidence that the Hurrians engaged in any large scale building activities throughout the Near East, it is quite possible that the Israelites simply attributed to them the works of the Sumerians of whom they had no memory. After all, the Hurrians were still around at the time the Genesis was written (c. 950 B.C.) but the Sumerians had completely disappeared nearly a thousand years previously.

It is then quite likely that the early Hungarians acquired Nimrod as their ancestor from a Hurrian upper class, which subsequently became completely assimilated among them and lost its ethnic identity. The memory of Nimrod, however, was preserved by the leaders of the people and when the Huns appeared on the scene, they were added as another son, thus integrating them in an age-old legend antedating their arrival by many centuries.

Nimrod's connection with the Hurrians is confirmed by the most ancient traditions of the Armenians relating to a legendary fight between their eponymous ancestor, Haik, and Nimrod.[39] It is reasonably clear that the *coup de grâce* to the declining Urartian kingdom was administered by the invading Armenians,[40] and it is highly probable, therefore, that Nimrod represents Urartu in the legendary fight referred to. Indeed, the memory of this struggle may have been originally preserved in the writings of the Urartians whence the Armenians adopted it after attaining literacy.[41]

Having first identified Nimrod's sons, we have now found the father himself. He was a Hurrian, the foremost potentate on earth in his time and a mighty hunter before the Lord. It was he who set off the Hungarians on their long journey through history which took them to the Caucasus and later on to the Carpathian Basin. Kézai may now rest in peace: his genealogy of the Magyars has been proved correct and impeccable beyond reasonable doubt.

CHAPTER 9

A New Hungarian Prehistory

The past is immutable because it has already happened but our understanding of it changes continuously. The divers origins attributed to Hungarians have undergone many changes in the past and we cannot expect the views outlined in this book to remain uncorrected over the years to come. What we hope to have achieved, however, is to give a new direction to the search for truth in Hungarian prehistory. Let us now summarise our findings.

Hungarians emerge from the darkness of early prehistory as an independent branch of the peoples speaking the present Ural-Altaic languages. It seems that some 10,000 years ago, or even earlier, they lived in an area also occupied by the ancestors of the Finno-Ugrian peoples and the Sumerians. The geographical position and precise time slot of this cohabitation cannot be determined in our present state of knowledge.

From the first half of the fourth millenium B.C. and most likely even a millenium earlier, the proto-Magyars appear as part of the Subarians living in Upper Mesopotamia and the region between the Tigris and the Zagros mountains. For a period of nearly two thousand years, they are subject to strong Sumerian linguistic and cultural influences, accompanied by some degree of ethnic intermingling. At the beginning of the second millenium B.C., they are swept to the north by the turbulence caused by the Hurrians and are settled in Transcaucasia as frontier guardsmen.

From c. 1800 B.C. until c. 1300 B.C., the proto-Magyars, now separated from their Subarian milieu, form themselves into a distinct nation in Transcaucasia under the rule of a Hurrian upper class. This upper stratum becomes entirely submerged during the following five centuries, when the Magyars assume independent existence as masters of their own destiny. In the eighth and seventh centuries B.C., they come again under late Hurrian (Urartian) hegemony for a short time but their association with the kingdom of Urartu is only of a loose nature and they soon reassert their independence.

Around the sixth century B.C., the Magyars probably receive their first infusion of Turkic blood by mixing with a branch of the Scythians. About the second century B.C., a branch of the Huns settles in the Caucasus and for the next six hundred years the Magyars mix with them so thoroughly that they merge into one nation. In the process, the Huns become the politically dominant element but they assume the language and identity of the Magyars and, as a unified people, they achieve a position of pre-eminence among the other Hunnish and Turkic peoples in the area.

In the fifth century A.D., this Hun-Magyar amalgam splits into three parts: one remains in Transcaucasia, one shifts gradually to the north and the main body sets out in a western direction, ending its journey in present-day Hungary at the end of the ninth century.

Whilst the writer regards the main aspects of this brief sketch as clearly established or at least strongly indicated by the facts known to us at this stage, there are many details which require further investigation. The language or languages of the Subarians will have to be studied and properly classified. More precise analyses of Sumerian-Hungarian linguistic affiliations will have to be carried out, with particular regard to the traces left in Hungarian by the various stages of development and dialects of the Sumerian language. The possibility of Hurrian loanwords in Hungarian will have to be investigated. The same goes for possible Hittite and Armenian influences. Archaeological studies will have to be made in various areas of Mesopotamia, Subartu and Transcaucasia with a view to determining the presence and successive stages of development of the early Magyars. Sumerian, Akkadian, Assyrian, Persian and other Near Eastern sources will have to be re-examined for possible references to the Hungarians and their history. In other words, all our researches into Hungarian prehistory will have to be reorientated and proceed on the basis of fresh assumptions.

A New Hungarian Prehistory

It is the firm conviction of the writer that the speculative character and high degree of uncertainty, not to speak of obvious untruths and deliberate distortions, manifest in most works dealing with the origin of the Magyars over the last two hundred years is largely due to the fact that our historians have been looking in the wrong direction. They have tried to find the Magyars in places where they have never been. The Magyars themselves have never claimed to have lived in those places: it was the speculation of linguists which put them there. No wonder the present state of Hungarian prehistory is so unsatisfactory.

Let us look boldly and with unbiased eyes at the area where Kézai placed the ancestral home of the Magyars: the region of Persia and beyond. Let us set out on a pilgrimage to those ancient lands in our search for the truth. The writer is confident that we shall not be deceived.

There will be many centuries to go through and the going will be often rough. There will be gaps here and there, dark ages and inconsistent reports. We will stumble at times and we may hesitate and even follow dead-end paths at the crossroads of history. But the journey will be worthwhile. It will lead us to truth.

And there, at the end of the road, Nimrod, the mighty hunter, awaits us with a kindly smile.

Notes

CHAPTER 1

THE NATIONAL TRADITION

1. Gy. Németh, *A magyar rovásirás*, Budapest, 1934.
2. B. Hóman, *Magyar Történet*, Budapest, 1941, Vol. I, p. 112. The chronicler known as Anonymus (see p. 3) also refers to these, albeit with contempt, and states (42, 324) that the peasants and players 'fortia facta et bella Hungarorum usque in hodiernum diem obliuioni non tradunt'.
3. Anonymus states in the introduction to his *Gesta Hungarorum*: Et si tam nobilissima gens Hungarie primordia sue generationis et fortia queque facta ex falsis fabulis rusticorum uel a garrulo cantu ioculatorum quasi sompniando audiret ualde indecorum et satis indecens esset.
4. B. Hóman, 'La première période de l'historiographie hongroise', *Revue des études hongroises*, Vol. III (1925), p. 125, at p. 133.
5. Hóman, 'La première période de l'historiographie hongroise', p. 135.
6. B. Hóman, *A Szent László-kori Gesta Ungarorum és XII-XIII századi leszármazói*, Budapest, 1925. The conclusions reached by Hóman in this work were repeated by him in a summary form in his 'La première période de l'historiographie hongroise', supra.
7. Hóman, *A Szent László-kori Gesta Ungarorum*, supra.
8. C. A. Macartney, *The medieval Hungarian historians*, Cambridge, 1953, pp. 34-36.
9. Macartney, op. cit., p. 59.
10. Macartney, op. cit., p. 63; Hóman, 'La première période de l'historiographie hongroise', p. 158; Denis Sinor, *History of Hungary*, London, 1959, pp. 55-56.
11. Hóman, 'La première période de l'historiographie hongroise', p. 158.
12. 'Tunc elegerunt sibi querere terram Pannonie quam audiuerant fama uolante terram Athile regis esse de cuius progenie dux Almus pater Arpad descenderat.' Anonymus, 5, 53.
13. Anonymus, 46, 361. The ruins Anonymus describes were in fact those of Aquincum, a Roman city on the site of the present Obuda, a north-western suburb of Budapest.

Notes

14. Hóman, *Magyar Történet,* Vol. I, pp. 70-74.
15. Gotfried of Viterbo who was a contemporary of Anonymus, writes in his *Pantheon* (c. 1190) that 'quia Gothorum gens ex Magog filio Japhet filii Noe orta est affirmat chronica ipsorum Gothorum'. The reference is obviously to the *Historia Gothorum* of Isidore of Seville (c. 560-636) where a similar statement occurs.
16. Isidore of Seville writes in his *Originum seu Etymologiarum libri:* 'Scythia sicut et Gothia a Magog filio Japhet fertur cognominata'.
17. Anonymus, 3, 40; 14, 139.
18. 'Gens itaque Hungarorum fortissima et bellorum laboribus potentissima ut superius diximus de gente Scythica que per ydioma suum proprium Dentumoger dicitur duxit originem.' Anonymus, 5, 50.
19. Hóman, *Magyar Történet,* Vol. I, p. 66. There are two answers to this suggestion. Firstly, the ancient Magyars — and Anonymus himself — called the Don Etil or Etul (see C. A. Macartney, *The Magyars in the ninth century,* 1930, p. 53.). They therefore could not possibly have called it Den or Don 'in their own language' ('per ydioma suum proprium' — see note 18). Secondly, the etymology 'Den-tu-Magyar' does not make sense in Hungarian. One can sit at the 'tu' (modern *tö*) of a tree or even a mountain but not of a river. The mouth of a river is called in old Hungarian *torok* (cf. Zsitvatorok).
20. This explanation was given to me by Professor Ferenc Eckhart in the course of his lectures at the University of Budapest in 1940-41. I am not aware whether he ever expressed this view in writing.
21. He states in one passage (42, 325-6) that he did not include the story of how Botond knocked a hole in the golden gate of Constantinople 'quia in nullo codice hystoriographorum inueni nisi ex falsis fabulis rusticorum audiui'.
22. L. Juhász, *P. Magister, Gesta Hungarorum,* Budapest, 1932, p. 4; Macartney, *The medieval Hungarian historians,* p. 36.
23. Macartney, *The medieval Hungarian historians,* p. 89.
24. Béla IV, Ladislas' grandfather, settled a substantial body of Cumans in the Great Hungarian Plain following the Mongol invasion in 1241-42. These Cumans were a Turkic race who inhabited the western regions of the Ukraine and eastern Romania (in present-day terms) prior to their settlement in Hungary. Ladislas' mother was a Cuman princess and he spent a great deal of his time with his Cuman subjects. The Cumans were still largely pagans at that time and Ladislas' way of living was con-

sidered so scandalous by the Christian West that the Pope placed Hungary under an interdict several times because of his conduct.

25. It is unlikely that Kézai ever read Orosius who wrote around 415 but he probably picked up his references to the Huns in Jordanes (see the text comparisons between Jordanes and Kézai in Hóman, *A Szent László-kori Gesta Ungarorum*, p. 55-56).

26. J. Deér, *Pogány magyarság, keresztény magyarság*, Budapest, 1938, p. 236.

27. Macartney, *The medieval Hungarian historians*, p. 111.

28. Macartney, op. cit., p. 133.

29. C. A. Macartney, *The origin of the Hun Chronicle and Hungarian historical sources*, Oxford, 1951. See also Deér, op. cit., pp. 232 and ff.

30. Macartney, *The medieval Hungarian historians*, p. 38.

31. It is sufficient to cite Thomas of Spalato (c. 1260), a Croatian prelate who must have been otherwise fairly well disposed towards the Hungarians because at that time Croatia had already been under the Hungarian Crown for some hundred and seventy years, and nineteen years previously the King of Hungary (who was still reigning when Thomas wrote) actually took refuge in Croatia from the Mongol onslaught. He writes in his *Historia Salonitanorum pontificum atque Spalatensium:* 'Erant enim pagani crudelissimi, prius vocabuntur Huni, postea sunt Hungari nuncupati. Ante ipsa tempora dux Attila, ferocissimus persecutor christianorum, de predicta regione dicitur fuisse egressus.'

32. It is worth noting that at least one English historian has suggested that the Hungarian tradition embodied in the Nimrod-legend may be independent of the Mosaic tradition: see C. Townley-Fullam, 'Magyar Origins', *Westminster Review*, Vol. 176 (1911), p. 52, at p. 55.

33. Gerhard von Rad, *Genesis*, 1972, p. 25.

34. Von Rad, op. cit., p. 146.

35. B. Vawter, *A path through Genesis*, 1964, p. 101.

36. Vawter, op. cit., p. 101.

37. L. Cottrell, *The land of Shinar*, London, 1965, p. 14.

38. Cottrell, op. cit., p. 13.

39. Vawter, op. cit., p. 101.

40. *Encyclopaedia Britannica*, 1961, sub-tit. 'Babel'.

41. Cottrell, op. cit., p. 13.

42. J. B. Segal, *Edessa 'the blessed city'*, Oxford, 1970, pp. 1-3.

43. I. Bobula, *Kétezer magyar név sumir eredete*, Montreal, 1970, p, 5.

44. Bobula, op. cit., p. 5.
45. *The Illustrated Chronicle* also refers to Evilath but as Magog's place of abode, quoting the chronicle of Saint Sigilbert, Bishop of Antioch, as its source. However, no such bishop or chronicle is known: see *Képes Krónika*, Budapest, 1964, Vol. II, p. 187.
46. E. Herzfeld, *The Persian Empire*, Wiesbaden, 1968, p. 105.
47. Gy. László, *Hunor és Magyar nyomában*, Budapest, pp. 15-17, 51-52.
48. László, op. cit., p. 16.
49. László, op. cit., pp. 16-18.
50. László, op. cit., pp. 51-52; S. Zichy, 'The origins of the Magyar people', *A companion to Hungarian studies*, Budapest, 1943, pp. 15 and ff., at p. 19.
51. C. A. Macartney, *The Magyars in the ninth century*, Cambridge, 1930, pp. 87-90.
52. László, op. cit., pp. 64-66.

CHAPTER 2
EARLY FOREIGN SOURCES

1. All my references to the *Poveshti Yearbook* and subsequent Ukrainian and Russian chronicles are from A. Hodinka's bilingual (Slavic and Hungarian) edition, *Az orosz évkönyvek magyar vonatkozásai*, Budapest, 1916.
2. Gy. László, 'A 'kettös honfoglalás'-ról', *Archaeologiai Ertesitö*, Budapest, Vol. 97 (1970), pp. 161-187, at pp. 170 and 183; G. Fehér, 'A bolgár-törökök kapcsolatai a magyarsággal és a legujabb magyar östörténetkutatás', *Századok*, Budapest, 1935, pp. 513-53, at p. 548. In the terminology of the old Hungarians and their near relatives, 'white' meant the northern and 'black' the southern branch of the same thing. In this sense, 'white' and 'black' were applied not only to branches of the same people but also to rivers and even seas: cf. White Tisza, Black Tisza, White Körös, Black Körös, White Sea, Black Sea.
3. *Susdal Yearbook* ad ann. 1149 and 1152; *Moscow Chronicle*, ad ann. 1118 and 1151; *Tverj Yearbook*, ad ann. 1123 1151 and 1152 and *Halych-Volodymir Yearbook* from 1188 to 1286 inclusive (numerous references).
4. This view is confirmed by a third reference to 'mountains of the Ugors' in the *Poveshti Yearbook* under the year 898 where it is stated that before arriving under Kiev, 'the Ugri crossed the

mountains still today called the mountains of the Ugri'. What mountains this refers to is not altogether clear but the reference, when coupled with the subsequent reference to the Carpathians under the same name, makes it obvious that from the viewpoint of the Kievan chroniclers, the mountains of the Ugri were always mountains which had to be crossed by the Hungarians on their way to the west. Indeed, the successive references to 'the mountains of the Ugri' in three different locations almost make the mountains themselves move from the Caucasus to the Carpathians in the footsteps of the Magyars.

5. C. A. Macartney, *The Magyars in the ninth century,* Cambridge, 1930; p. 71; S. Zichy, 'The origins of the Magyar people', *A companion to Hungarian studies,* Budapest, 1943, p. 17.

6. Zichy, op. cit., p. 17; see also Macartney, op. cit., p. 71.

7. Priscus Rhetor, *Historia,* ed. Bonn, p. 158.

8. Priscus Rhetor, op. cit., p. 158.

9. *Die sogenannte Kirchengeschichte des Zacharias Rhetor,* ed. K. Ahrens and G. Krüger, Leipzig, 1899, p. 382.

10. B. Munkácsi, 'Az "ugor" népnév eredete', *Ethnographia,* Vol. VI (1895), reprinted in *Magyar Történelmi Szemle,* Vol. II (1971), pp. 1-39.

11. A number of Hungarian historians interpret *ogur* as meaning 'arrow' in western Turkic languages, now lost, and consider that in the composite forms in which it appears, this word signifies 'tribe'; thus, *on-ogur,* ten tribes: see e.g., B. Hóman, *Magyar Történet,* Budapest, 1941, Vol. I, p. 634; S. Zichy, op. cit., p. 29. However, the western Turkic word for 'arrow' is *ok,* not *ogur:* see Gy. Németh, *A honfoglaló magyarság kialakulása,* Budapest, 1930, p. 41. As Munkácsi has demonstrated in the article cited above, *ugor* is definitely the name of a people and *ogur* is simply a variant of that name. Whilst I do not agree with all of Munkácsi's conclusions, I consider that on this point he is clearly right.

12. Most Hungarian historians consider that the various names by which the Magyars are called in western European languages — Hungarian, Ungar, hongrois, etc. — are derived from the name Onogur and argue on this basis that they must have formed part of the Onogur federation for a considerable time. There are two main reason why this theory must be wrong. Firstly, the Ugors are mentioned as a people separate from the Onogurs in a number of Byzantine and other sources and when these sources first identify the Hungarians, they call them Ugors and not Onogurs.

Notes

Secondly, in addition to the Ukrainians, Russians and Byzantines, a number of other surrounding nations also called the Magyars by the name Ugor or similar names, e.g., *ugar, ugrin* (Serb); *ugrin* (Bulgarian); *uher* (Czech); *uher* (Slovak). The addition of an *n* (so as to make Ungor out of Ugor) was therefore a corruption and had nothing to do with Onogur. This is confirmed by the concurrent use of *Ungri* and *Agareni* in the St Gallen Annals. See also H. Grégoire, 'Le nom des hongrois', *Byzantion*, Bruxelles, Vol. 12 (1937), pp. 645-650, where the suggestion is made that some of the Slavs may have mispronounced the Greek *uggroi* for *Vangar-Vengry*. It follows from all this that rather than assuming the name of the Onogurs, it was the Magyars who gave their name, in a composite form, to the former, suggesting that the Magyars were the more prominent of the two and probably supplied the ruling class or upper ethnic stratum of the Onogurs.

13. K. Hannestad, 'Les relations de Byzance avec la Transcaucasie et l'Asie Central aux 5e et 6e siècles', *Byzantion*, Bruxelles, Vols. 25-26-27 (1955-56-57), pp. 421-56, at p. 443.
14. Agathias, *Epigrammata*, ed. Bonn, p. 146.
15. Theophanes, *Chronographia*, ed. Bonn, p. 270; Malalas, *Chronographia*, ed. Bonn, pp. 431-32. Malalas gives the names of the brothers as Grod and Mugel.
16. *Die sogenannte Kirchengeschichte des Zacharias Rhetor,* supra, p. 253; *The Syriac Chronicle known as that of Zachariah of Mitylene,* trans. F. J. Hamilton and E. W. Brooks, London, 1899.
17. Menander Protector, *Historia*, ed. Bonn, p. 301.
18. Theophylactes Simocatta, *Historia*, ed. Bonn, pp. 283-4.
19. Munkácsi, op. cit., p. 20. This again demonstrates the antiquity and eminence of the people called Ugor.
20. 'Hostes illis populis inexperti qui Ugri vocantur.' My quotation from Macartney, *The Magyars in the ninth century*, p. 71.
21. J. Duft, *Die Ungarn in Sankt Gallen*, Zürich, 1957, pp. 10-13 and 57.
22. 'Ugri qui sua lingua sunt Maegeri.' My quotation from C. A. Macartney, *The origin of the Hun Chronicle and Hungarian historical sources*, Oxford, 1951, p. 51.
23. Macartney, *The Magyars in the ninth century*, pp. 29-31.
24. Macartney, *The Magyars in the ninth century*, p. 63; B. Hóman, 'Les récentes études relatives à l'origine du peuple hongrois', *Revue des études hongroises et finno-ougriennes*, Vol. II (1924), pp. 156-71, at p. 161.

25. Theophanes, *Chronographia,* ed. Bonn, p. 545.
26. Constantinus Porphyrogenetus, *De Thematibus,* ed. Bonn, p. 46. Constantinus actually uses the name 'Onogundur', the same as Theophanes before him, which is probably derived from the Turkic plural of Onogur: see Munkácsi, op. cit., p. 22.
27. *Die sogenannte Kirchengeschichte des Zacharias Rhetor,* supra, p. 253.
28. V. Minorsky, 'Une nouvelle source persane sur les Hongrois au Xe siècle', *Nouvelle revue de Hongrie,* Vol. 56 (1937), p. 305, at p. 310.
29. Belgrade (which means 'white castle' in the Southern Slav languages) was indifferently called Bolgárfehérvár (Bulgar white castle) and Nándorfehérvár ('Nándor' white castle) by the mediaeval Hungarians.
30. The role played by the Hungarians in the story of the rape — being the raper and not the raped one — again confirms that they must have been in a superior position towards the Onogurs and Bulgars.
31. Constantinus Porphyrogenetus, *De administrando imperio,* ed. Gy. Moravcsik and R. J. H. Jenkins, Budapest, 1949.
32. Constantinus Porphyrogenetus, op. cit., Vol. I, pp. 172-73.
33. Constantinus Porphyrogenetus, op. cit., Vol. II, pp. 147-48; Macartney, *The Magyars in the ninth century,* p. 79.
34. Constantinus Porphyrogenetus, op. cit., Vol. II, p. 147; Macartney, *The Magyars in the ninth century,* pp. 87-90; see also Gy. László, *Hunor és Magyar nyomában,* Budapest, 1967, pp. 66, 90.
35. Constantinus Porphyrogenetus, op. cit., c. 38.
36. Gy. László, *A honfoglalókról,* Budapest, 1973, p. 20.
37. Constantinus Porphyrogenetus, op. cit., c. 40.
38. L. Halphen, *Les barbares,* Paris, 1930, p. 9.
39. K. Hannestad, op. cit.
40. Theophylactes Simocatta, *Historia,* II, 18, ed. Bonn, p. 105.
41. Agathias, *Epigrammata,* ed. Bonn, p. 105.
42. Procopius Caesareensis, *Gotthica Historia,* ed. Grotius, pp. 410, 453.
43. *Herodotus,* tr. A. D. Godley, London, 1926, II, 104; III, 94; VII, 78.
44. Xenophon, *Expeditio Cyri (Anabasis)* ed. C. Hude, Leipzig, 1972, Book IV, chapters 7 and 8.
45. A. Pretor, *The Anabasis of Xenophon,* Cambridge, 1881, Vol. II, p. 454

46. W. W. How and J. Wells, *A commentary on Herodotus,* Oxford, 1950, Vol. I, p. 286.

47. It is noteworthy that in the early tenth century Byzantine life of St Clement, the Hungarians raiding Bulgaria are referred to as Makair Scythians (Macartney, *The Magyars in the ninth century,* p. 129). At the very least, this shows that the Greeks were always inclined to render the name Magyar in this form. The possibility that the Makrones were Magyars has already been raised by V. Padányi, *Dentumagyaria,* Buenos Aires, 1963, pp. 242-43. I would go further than he and consider the identity of these two peoples highly probable.

48. *Encyclopaedia Britannica,* 1961, sub-tit. 'Colchis'.

49. C. A. Macartney, *The origin of the Hun Chronicle and Hungarian historical sources,* Oxford, 1951, p. 79. The St Gallen annals refer to the Magyars as Huns at the time of their first attack on the eastern Frankish empire in 862: see J. Duft, *Die Ungarn in Sankt Gallen,* p. 10.

50. C. A. Macartney, *The origin of the Hun Chronicle,* p. 156; same author, *The Magyars in the ninth century,* p. 156.

51. *Herodotus,* I, 72; II, 104.

52. Macartney, *The origin of the Hun Chronicle,* pp. 9, 113.

CHAPTER 3

FISH-SMELLING RELATIONS

1. 'Nam cum una et eadem de generatione a quodam scilicet Hunnor et Magor unanimiter processerint': Werböczi, *Tripartitum opus juris consuetudinarii inclyti regni Hungariae,* I, 3, para. 5.

2. B. Hóman, 'Les récentes études relatives à l'origine du peuple hongrois', *Revue des études hongroises et finno-ougriennes,* Vol. II (1924), pp. 156-71, at pp. 156-57.

3. B. Hóman, *Magyar Történet,* Budapest, 1936, Vol. V, pp. 279-81.

4. Pray, op. cit., I, 1.

5. I wish to state categorically that I have no desire to cast any aspersions on Finns, Estonians and related peoples whose heroism and high achievements in the face of overwhelming odds are well known. However, the fact remains that the relationship between these peoples and Hungarians is extremely remote.

6. J. Szinnyei, 'L'académie hongroise des sciences et la linguistique

hongroise', *Revue des études hongroises et finno-ougriennes*, Vol. III (1925), pp. 41-61, at pp. 45-46.

7. See the biographical notes in *Az ösi magyar hitvilág*, ed. V. Diószegi, Budapest, 1971, pp. 431-32.

8. The contents of this and the following three paragraphs are based on Szinnyei's rather revealing article cited under 6.

9. This family of languages comprises the Finno-Ugrian and Samoy-edic languages (jointly called the Uralic group) and the Turkic, Mongolian and Manchu-Tungus languages (called the Altaic group).

10. P. Hunfalvy, *Magyarország ethnographiája*, Budapest, 1876.

11. H. Vámbéry, *Der Ursprung der Magyaren*, Leipzig, 1882, p. VII.

12. Szinnyei, op. cit., pp. 59-60; E. Zichy, 'L'origine du peuple hongrois', *Revue des études hongroises et finno-ougriennes*, Vol. I (1923), pp. 5-14, notes on pp. 8 and 9.

13. *Finn-magyar szótár*, Budapest, 1884; *Magyar nyelvhasonlitás*, Budapest, 1894, and several editions thereafter.

14. J. Szinnyei, *A magyarok eredete és ösi müveltsége*, Budapest, 1908; same author, *Die Herkunft der Ungarn*, Berlin, 1923.

15. 'A magyarság östörténete és müveltsége a honfoglalásig,' *Magyar nyelvtudomány kézikönyve*, Budapest, 1923, Vol. I, 5. Zichy summarised his main conclusions in his article 'L'origine du peuple hongrois', cited under 12.

16. Twenty years later, Zichy made a complete about-face and declared that Hungarians were a Turkic people which somehow had acquired a Finno-Ugrian idom: see S. Zichy, 'The origins of the Magyar people', *A companion to Hungarian studies*, Budapest, 1943, pp. 15-47.

17. A. Sauvageot, 'L'origine du peuple hongrois', *Revue des études hongroises et finno-ougriennes*, Vol. II (1924), pp. 106-16, at p. 114.

18. A. M. Tallgren, sub-tit. 'Finno-Ugrier', *Reallexikon der Vorge-schichte*, ed. Max Ebert, Berlin, 1925, Vol. 3, p. 354.

19. K. B. Wiklund, sub-tit. 'Finno-Ugrier', *Reallexikon der Vorge-schichte*, Vol. 3, p. 376.

20. B. Hóman, 'Les récentes études relatives à l'origine du peuple hongrois', loc. cit., pp. 158-59; Sauvageot, op. cit., p. 110.

21. See e.g., M. Zsirai, *Finnugor rokonságunk*, Budapest, 1937; P. Hajdu, 'The origins of Hungarian', *The Hungarian language*, ed. L. Benkö and S. Imre, *Janua Linguarum, Series Practica 134*, 1972, pp. 29 and ff.

Notes

22. Gy. László, 'A "kettös honfoglalás"-ról', *Archaeologiai Ertesitö,* Budapest, Vol. 97 (1970), pp. 161-87, at p. 161.

23. Gy. László, *Östörténetünk legkorábbi szakaszai,* Budapest, 2nd ed., 1971, p. 190.

24. For an exposition of this theory, see P. Hajdu, 'The origins of Hungarian', loc. cit.; A. Sauvageot, *Les anciens finnois,* Paris, 1961, pp. 25-29; K. B. Wiklund, sub-tit. 'Finno-Ugrier', *Reallexikon der Vorgeschichte,* Vol. 3, pp. 364-79; Gy. László, *Östörténetünk legkorábbi szakaszai,* pp. 33-35.

25. Gy. László, *Östörténetünk legkorábbi szakaszai,* p. 35.

26. László, op. cit., p. 37; 'The Hungarian language' (by S. Imre), *Information Hungary,* ed. F. Erdei, 1968, p. 55.

27. *Information Hungary,* p. 56.

28. *Information Hungary,* p. 55.

29. D. Sinor, 'Történelmi hipotézis a magyar nyelv történetében', *Nyelvtudományi értekezések,* No. 58 (1967), pp. 195-200.

30. Vámbéry, *Der Ursprung der Magyaren,* pp. 200 and ff. and Appendix IV.

31. S. Csöke, *Szumir-magyar egyeztetö szótár,* Buenos Aires, 1970, pp. 166-92; same author, *A sumir ösnyelvtöl a magyar élönyelvig,* New York, 1969.

32. B. Collinder, *Fenno-ugric vocabularly,* Stockholm, 1955.

33. Gy. László, op. cit., p. 37.

34. E.g., *kar* (arm), *gyomor* (stomach), *szakáll* (beard), *térd* (knee), *köldök* (navel). Sinor observes somewhat cynically that if the method of drawing conclusions of a cultural and social nature from the derivation of various words in the Hungarian language is a valid one — a practice indulged in by Szinnyei, Zichy, Zsirai and many others — then it may also be argued that the Hungarians had no stomachs or knees before their contacts with the Turco-Bulgars!

35. S. Csöke, *Szumir-magyar egyeztetö szótár,* supra.

36. Vámbéry, op. cit., pp. 211-20; S. Csöke, *A sumir ösnyelvtöl a magyar élönyelvig,* supra.

37. Vámbéry, op. cit., pp. 205-11.

38. G. Bárczi, 'The Hungarian language', *A companion to Hungarian studies,* Budapest, 1943, pp. 272-84, at p. 272.

39. B. Munkácsi, *Arja és kaukázusi elemek a finn-magyar nyelvekben,* Budapest, 1901; same author, 'Asszir nyomok a finn-magyar nyelvekben', *Magyar Nyelvör,* Budapest, 1911.

40. Bárczi, op. cit., p. 279.

41. Wiklund, loc. cit.; László, op. cit., 194.
42. T. Vuorela, *The Finno-Ugric peoples*, Indiana University, 1964, p. 305.
43. A. Sauvageot, *Les anciens finnois*, p. 13.
44. Gy. Németh, *A honfoglaló magyarság kialakulása*, Budapest, 1930, pp. 124-25; J. Deér, *Pogány magyarság, keresztény magyarság*, Budapest, 1938, p. 37.
45. P. Lipták, 'Anthropologische Beiträge zum Problem der Ethnogenesis der Altungarn', *Acta Archaeologica Academiae Scientiarum Hungaricae*, Vol. I (1951), pp. 231-46, at pp. 243-45.
46. Lipták, op. cit., pp. 241-42.
47. Hajdu, op. cit., p. 16.
48. Wiklund, loc. cit.
49. Deér, op. cit., p. 38.
50. Hajdu, op. cit., p. 29.
51. G. Bárczi, *Magyar hangtörténet*, 2nd ed., Budapest, 1958, p. 6.
52. Gy. László, *A honfoglalókról*, Budapest, 1973, p. 16.
53. László, *A honfoglalókról*, p. 20.
54. Tallgren, loc. cit., pp. 354-64; Gy. László, *Hunor és Magyar nyomában*, Budapest, 1967, pp. 91-92.
55. Tallgren, loc. cit., p. 360.
56. C. A. Macartney, *The Magyars in the ninth century*, Cambridge, 1930, p. 33; László, *A honfoglalókról*, p. 36.
57. Macartney, op. cit., p. 63; B. Munkácsi, 'A magyar öshaza kérdése', reprinted in *A finnugor öshaza nyomában*, ed. J. Kodolányi Jr., Budapest, 1973, at p. 217; and many others.
58. F. Haensell, *Probleme der Vor-Völker-Forschung (Grundzüge einer ethnologischen Urgeschichte)*, Frankfurt/Main-Wien, 1955, pp. 226-27.
59. B. Gunda, 'Ethnography', *A companion to Hungarian studies*, Budapest, 1943, pp. 285-304, at p. 286.
60. Gy. László, *A honfoglalókról*, p. 46; B. Szabolcsi, 'A survey of Hungarian music', *A companion to Hungarian studies*, Budapest, 1943, pp. 468-85, at pp. 469-70.
61. László, *Östörténetünk legkorábbi szakaszai*, p. 20.
62. L. Bartucz, 'La composition anthropologique du peuple hongrois', *Revue des études hongroises et finno-ougriennes*, Paris, Vol. 5 (1927), pp. 209-41; same author, 'A magyarság faji összetétele', *Magyar Statisztikai Szemle*, Budapest, Vol. 17 (1939), pp. 337-49.
63. J. Nemeskéri, 'Anthropologie des conquérants hongrois', *Revue d'histoire comparée*, 1947, pp. 174-80.

64. P. Lipták, 'Anthropologische Beiträge zum Problem der Ethnogenesis der Altungarn', supra; same author, 'Die Entstehung des ungarischen Volkes auf Grund anthropologischer Funde', *Homo, Zeitschrift für die vergleichende Forschung am Menschen,* Göttingen, Vol. 21 (1970), pp. 197-209.
65. Roland B. Dixon, *The racial history of man,* New York, 1923, pp. 129-31.
66. Haensell, op. cit., p. 227; cf. Dixon, op. cit., pp. 475 and ff.

CHAPTER 4

A RACE OF TURKS

1. C. A. Macartney, *The Magyars in the ninth century,* Cambridge, 1930, pp. 5 and ff., quotation from p. 206.
2. Macartney, op. cit., pp. 6 and ff., quotation from pp. 206 and 209.
3. S. Zichy, 'The origins of the Magyar people', *A companion to Hungarian studies,* Budapest, 1943, pp. 15-47.
4. B. Hóman, 'Les récentes études relative à l'origine du peuple hongrois', *Revue des études hongroises et finno-ougriennes,* Paris, Vol. II (1924), pp. 156-71, at pp. 157-58; E. Zichy, 'L'origine du peuple hongrois', same review, Vol. I (1923), pp. 5-14, at p. 6.
5. L. Szalay, *Magyarország története,* Leipzig, 1852, Vol. I, p. 4.
6. H. Marczali, 'A magyarok östörténete a honfoglalásig', *A magyar nemzet története,* ed. S. Szilágyi, Budapest, 1895, Vol. I, pp. 7-15.
7. Z. Gombocz, *Die bulgarisch-türkischen Lehnwörter in der ungarischen Sprache, Mémoires de la Sociéte Finno-Ougrienne,* XXX, Helsinki, 1912.
8. Gombocz, op. cit., pp. 187, 208.
9. Gombocz, op. cit., p. 193.
10. Gombocz, 'Az igék átvételéről', *Nyelvör* XXX, pp. 105-09.
11. Sulán, 'A kétnyelvüség néhány kérdéséhez', *Magyar Nyelv* LIX, pp. 253-65; see also M. K. Palló, 'Zu den ältesten alttürkischen verbalen Entlehnungen der ungarischen Sprache', *Acta Orientalia Acad. Scient. Hungaricae,* Vol. 20 (1967), pp. 111-18.
12. Gombocz, *Die bulgarisch-türkischen Lehnwörter in der ungarischen Sprache,* loc. cit., pp. 191, 205-06. It is noteworthy, however, that even in this early work, Gombocz expressly left open the possibility of a southern *Urheimat* of the Hungarians (at p. 205).

13. Gombocz, 'A bolgárkérdés és a magyar hunmonda', *Magyar Nyelv*, 1921, pp. 15-21.
14. Hóman, 'Les récentes études relative à l'origine du peuple hongrois', loc. cit., p. 160.
15. J. Gesztesi, 'L'origine des hongrois', *Revue mondiale*, Paris, Vol. 173 (1927), pp. 61-67, at p. 66.
16. See e.g. B. Hóman, *Magyar Történet*, Budapest, 1941, Vol. I; J. Deér, *Pogány magyarság, keresztény magyarság*, Budapest, 1938.
17. G. Bárczi, 'The Hungarian language', *A companion to Hungarian studies*, Budapest, 1943, pp. 272-84, at p. 274.
18. See e.g. Th. v. Bogyay, 'Nomaden-Kultur, Die Kultur der Ungarn', *Handbuch der Kulturgeschichte*, Frankfurt, 1961, Vol. II, p. 8.
19. Gy. László, 'A "kettös honfoglalás"-ról', *Archaeologiai Ertesitö*, Budapest, Vol. 97 (1970), pp. 161-87, at p. 186; same author, *A honfoglalókról*, Budapest, 1973, p. 21.
20. L. Benkö and S. Imre, *The Hungarian language, Janua Linguarum, Series Practica 134*, 1972, p. 30.
21. L. Bartucz, 'A magyarság faji összetétele', *Magyar Statisztikiai Szemle*, Budapest, Vol. 17 (1939), pp. 337-49; same author, 'Die Geschichte der Rassen in Ungarn und das Werden des heutigen ungarischen Volkskörpers', *Ungarische Jahrbücher*, Vol. 19 (1939), pp. 281-320; J. Nemeskéri, 'Anthropologie des conquérants hongrois', *Revue d'histoire comparée*, 1947, pp. 174-80; P. Lipták, 'Anthropologische Beiträge zum Problem der Ethnogenesis der Altungarn', *Acta Archaelogica Acad. Scient. Hung.*, Vol .I (1951), pp. 231-46; same author, 'Die Entstehung des ungarischen Volkes auf Grund anthropologischer Funde', *Homo, Zeitschrift für die vergleichende Forschung am Menschen*, Göttingen, Vol. 21 (1970), pp. 197-209.
22. Lipták, 'Die Entstehung des ungarischen Volkes auf Grund anthropologischer Funde', loc. cit., p. 206.
23. Bartucz, 'A magyarság faji öszetétele', loc. cit., p. 347. Bartucz considers that nearly 30 per cent of modern Hungarians belong to the Turanid type.
24. F. Eckhart, *Magyar alkotmány és jogtörténet*, Budapest, 1940.
25. B. Gunda, 'Ethnography', *A companion to Hungarian studies*, Budapest, 1943, pp. 285-304, at p. 287.
26. László, *A honfoglalókról*, p. 62.
27. N. Fettich, 'A levédiai magyarság a régészet megvilágitásában', *Századok*, Budapest, Vol. 67 (1933), pp. 369-99, at p. 399.
28. Gy. Németh, *A magyar rovásirás*, Budapest, 1934.

29. B. Szabolcsi, 'A survey of Hungarian music', *A companion to Hungarian studies*, Budapest, 1943, pp. 468-85, at p. 469.
30. László, *A honfoglalókról*, p. 46.
31. L. Vargyas, 'Ugor réteg a magyar népzenében', *Kodály Emlékkönyv*, Budapest, 1953, pp. 611-57.
32. Szabolcsi, op. cit., p. 469; Gombocz, *Die bulgarisch-türkischen Lehnwörter in der ungarischen Sprache*, supra, at p. 207.
33. S. Zichy, 'The origins of the Magyar people', *A companion to Hungarian studies*, Budapest, 1943, pp. 15-47, at p. 44.

CHAPTER 5

THE HUN BROTHERS

1. As to the Chinese sources referred to, see L. Hambis, 'Le problème des Huns', *Revue historique*, Paris, Vol. 220 (1958), pp. 249-70, at pp. 249-51.
2. Hambis, op. cit., p. 259; W. M. McGovern, *The early empires of Central Asia*, University of North Carolina, 1939, pp. 95-96.
3. McGovern, op. cit., p. 99.
4. Hambis, op. cit., pp. 260-61.
5. Hambis, op. cit., p. 260.
6. Hambis, op. cit., pp. 261-68.
7. F. Altheim, *Geschichte der Hunnen*, Berlin, 1959-62, Vol. I, p. 21.
8. Altheim, op. cit., Vol. I, pp. 7, 22; J. Wiesner, 'Die Kulturen der frühen Reitervölker', *Handbuch der Kulturgeschichte*, Frankfurt am Main, 1968, p. 147; McGovern, op. cit., pp. 96-99; Gy. Németh, *A honfoglaló magyarság kialakulása*, Budapest, 1930, pp. 127 and ff.
9. Altheim, op. cit., Vol. I, p. 3.
10. Wiesner, op. cit., p. 149; also Altheim, op. cit., Vol. I, p. 4.
11. Wiesner, op. cit., p. 149.
12. Altheim, op. cit., Vol. I, pp. 14-15.
13. Altheim, op. cit., Vol. I, p. 9.
14. Altheim, op. cit., Vol. I, p. 9.
15. Altheim, op. cit., Vol. I, pp. 12-13; Vol. IV, p. 28.
16. F. Altheim, 'Das Auftreten der Hunnen in Europa', *Acta Archaeologica Acad. Scient. Hung.*, Vol. II (1952), pp. 269-75.
17. K. Lukácsy, *A magyarok őselei, hajdankori nevei és lakhelyei, eredeti örmény kutfők után*, Kolozsvár, 1870, pp. 100-13. Lukácsy was a learned Armenian priest in Transylvania (then part

of Hungary) whose work contains a highly valuable examination of old Armenian sources relating to the Huns and other Turkic peoples usually connected with the Hungarians.

18. Altheim, *Geschichte der Hunnen*, Vol. I, pp. 57-8, Wiesner, op. cit., p. 149.
19. Altheim, op. cit., Vol. I, pp. 58-68.
20. As to the dates and events referred to in this paragraph, see K. Hannestad, 'Les relations de Byzance avec la Transcaucasie et l'Asie Centrale aux 5e et 6e siècles', *Byzantion*, Bruxelles, Vols. 25-27 (1955-57), pp. 421-56.
21. Altheim, op. cit., Vol. I, pp. 22, 83; Vol. IV, pp. 30-31; Hannestad, op. cit.; L. Halphen, *Les barbares*, Paris, 1930, pp. 33-34. Németh states (op. cit., p. 128), that he hardly knows any historian of renown outside Hungary who does not acknowledge the identity of Huns and Bulgars. Németh does not share this view, however, and argues that the Huns spoke a Turkish language different from that of the Bulgars.
22. Z. Gombocz, *Die bulgarisch-türkischen Lehnwörter in der ungarischen Sprache, Mémoires de la Société Finno-Ougrienne*, XXX, Helsinki, 1912.
23. Indeed, the idea that the Magyars were at some stage incorporated in the empire of the Huns is accepted by most modern historians.
24. Whilst the Hungarians were thus identified as Ugors to the outside world, it is quite probable that in their own language they continued to call themselves Magors or Magyars. In Chapter 8, we shall endeavour to resolve this apparent inconsistency of the same people being called by two different names at the same time.
25. The pre-1918 kingdom of Romania. Transylvania formed part of Hungary up to 1918.
26. C. A. Macartney, *The origin of the Hun Chronicle and Hungarian historical sources*, Oxford, 1951.
27. Macartney, op. cit., p. 9.
28. Gy. Németh, 'A székelyek eredetének kérdése', *Századok*, Vol. 69 (1935), pp. 129-56.
29. Németh, 'A székelyek eredetének kérdése', loc. cit., p. 155.
30. It is noteworthy that the Cumans who settled on the Great Hungarian Plains in 1242 (see note 24 to Chapter 1), retained their language for centuries and their language did not completely disappear until the eighteenth century.
31. Németh, 'A székelyek eredetének kérdése', loc. cit., p. 131.
32. Such a sudden literacy of a previously illiterate people of moun-

tain-dwellers, however, seems extremely unlikely. It is much more probable that the Szekelys brought their script with them from the Caucasus.

33. The main body of the Magyars, of course, having lived on the South Russian steppes for the subsequent five centuries, preferred the plains on their arrival in present-day Hungary.
34. Lukácsy, op. cit., pp. 172-75.
35. Lukácsy, op. cit., pp. 172-73.
36. Németh, *A honfoglaló magyarság kialakulása,* p. 219.

CHAPTER 6

THE PERSIAN CONNECTION

1. L. Benkö, 'The lexical stock of Hungarian', *The Hungarian language,* ed. L. Benkö and S. Imre, *Janua Linguarum, Series Practica 134,* 1972, pp. 177-78.
2. K. Lukácsy, *A magyarok öselei, hajdankori nevei és lakhelyei, eredeti örmény kutfök után,* Kolozsvár, 1870, p. 96.
3. H. Vámbéry, *Der Ursprung der Magyaren,* Leipzig, 1882, pp. 383-87.
4. Vámbéry, op. cit., p. 386.
5. B. Munkácsi, 'A magyar öshaza kérdése', *Ethnographia,* 1906, pp. 65-87.
6. N. Fettich, 'A levédiai magyarság a régészet megvilágitásában', *Századok,* Vol. 67 (1933), pp. 369-99, at p. 385.
7. I. Dienes, *A honfoglaló magyarok,* Budapest, 1972, at pp. 57-66.
8. Dienes, op. cit., p. 58.
9. Dienes, op. cit., p. 61.
10. A. Hekler, 'Die Kunst der ungarischen Landnahmezeit', *Acta Archaeologica,* Kopenhagen, Vol. 7 (1936), pp. 67-75.
11. N. Fettich, 'Adatok a honfoglaláskor archaeológiájához', *Archaeologiai Ertesitö,* Budapest, Vol. 45 (1931), pp. 48-112, at p. 105; Dienes, op. cit., Plates 63 and 64.
12. D. Dercsényi, 'Old Hungarian art', *A companion to Hungarian studies,* Budapest, 1943, pp. 415-47, at pp. 419-23; Hekler, op. cit., p. 75.
13. L. A. Mayer, *Saracenic heraldry,* Oxford, 1933, p. 9.
14. F. Badinyi Jós, 'A magyar nép legösibb nemeslevele', *Ausztráliai*

Sons of Nimrod

Magyar Kalendárium, 1966, pp. 33-44; J. Andrássy Kurta, 'Okori eredetü magyar emlékek', *Eletünk*, Szombathely, 1969, No. 1.
15. Woodward's *Treatise on heraldry*, 1892, p. 208.
16. Gy. László, *Hunor és Magyar nyomában*, Budapest, 1967, pp. 71-76.
17. László, op. cit., pp. 134-37; same author, *A honfoglalókról*, Budapest, 1973, p. 48.
18. I. Herényi, 'Válasz Kristó Gyula 'Bulcsu nemzetségének nyári szállása ürügyén' cimü hozzászólására', *Századok*, Vol. 106 (1972), pp. 1399-402. Herényi argues that the Hungarian chieftain Bulcsu was also of Iranian origin. Whilst this seems unlikely, he may have had a substantial Persian retinue.

CHAPTER 7

THE SUMERIANS

1. S. N. Kramer, *The Sumerians*, Chicago, 1963, pp. 42-43, 288.
2. A. Deimel, *Sumerische Grammatik*, Rome, 1939, pp. 1-2.
3. Deimel, op. cit., p. 2.
4. For the early history of the Sumerian controversy, see Zs. Varga, *Ötezer év távolából*, Debrecen, 1942, pp. 9-206 and I. Bobula, *Sumerian affiliations*, Washington, 1951, pp. 1-11.
5. Deimel, op. cit., p. 4; W. F. Albright and T. O. Lambdin, 'The evidence of language', *Cambridge Ancient History*, Revised edition, Fasc. 54, 1966, p. 33.
6. A number of Galgóczy's articles were recently republished in book form under the title 'J. Galgóczy, *A sumir kérdés*' in *Studia Sumiro-Hungarica*, Vol. 1, Gilgamesh, New York, 1968.
7. Republished in *Studia Sumiro-Hungarica*, Vol. 2, New York, 1968.
8. *Akadémiai-Ertesitö*, 1904, pp. 44-46; see also Varga, op. cit., pp. 113-15.
9. B. Munkácsi, 'Néhány szó a sumir rokonság védelméhez', *Ethnographia*, Vol. 15 (1904), pp. 147-54.
10. B. Munkácsi, 'A magyar öshaza kérdése', *Ethnographia*, 1906, pp. 65-87, reprinted in *A finnugor öshaza nyomában*, ed. J. Kodolányi Jr., Budapest, 1973, pp. 193-226. Munkácsi makes the important point that Hungarian has a number of extremely old Caucasian and Aryan loanwords which it acquired considerably earlier than its loanwords of Turkic origin. It is also noteworthy that he

attributes a substantial portion of the Aryan loanwords in Hungarian to Old Persian, Avesta, Middle Persian, Pamirian and Hindi influences.

11. B. Munkácsi, 'Asszir nyomok finn-magyar nyelvekben', *Magyar Nyelvör*, 1911, reprinted in *Magyar Öskutatás,* Buenos Aires, 1971, pp. 97-103.
12. I. Bobula, *A sumér-magyar rokonság kérdése,* Buenos Aires, 1961.
13. I. Bobula, *The origin of the Hungarian nation,* 1966; same author, *Kétezer magyar név sumir eredete,* Montreal, 1970.
14. S. Nagy, *A magyar nép kialakulásának története,* Buenos Aires, 1968.
15. S. Csöke, *Szumir-magyar egyeztetö szótár,* Buenos Aires, 1970; same author, *A sumér ösnyelvtöl a magyar élönyelvig,* New York, 1969.
16. A. Zakar, *A sumér nyelvröl,* Södertalje, 1970.
17. F. Badiny Jós, *Káldeától Ister-Gamig,* Buenos Aires, 1971; same author, *A sumir-magyar nyelvazonosság bizonyitó adatai,* Buenos Aires (undated); *Sumerian syntax and agglutination in Asian languages,* Canberra, 1971; *El pueblo de Nimrud,* Valparaiso, 1966; *A megtalált magyar östörténelem,* Sydney, 1967.
18. See W. F. Albright and T. O. Lambdin, op. cit., p. 33.
19. To be precise, *van* means 'is' in Hungarian but this does not make sense in a numeral.
20. I. Bobula, 'The Great Stag: A Sumerian divinity and its affiliations', *Anales de Historia Antigua y Medieval,* Buenos Aires, 1953, pp. 119-26.
21. B. Szabolcsi, 'The eastern relations of early Hungarian folk music', *Journal of the Royal Asiatic Society,* 1935, pp. 483-98, at p. 485.
22. Bobula, 'The Great Stag', supra.
23. Bobula, *A sumér-magyar rokonság kérdése,* pp. 71-82.
24. Bobula, *Sumerian affiliations,* p. 88.
25. This has been demonstrated by the researches of Andor Schedel of Budapest: see Badiny Jós, *Káldeától Ister-Gamig,* pp. 203-10.
26. L. Cottrell, *The land of Shinar,* London, 1965, p. 135.
27. A. Götze, *Hethiter, Churriter und Assyrer,* Oslo, 1936, p. 12; A. Moortgat, *Die Entstehung der sumerischen Hochkultur,* Leipzig, 1945, p. 11.

CHAPTER 8

SUBARTU AND THE HURRI PEOPLE

1. I. J. Gelb, *Hurrians and Subarians,* Chicago, 1944, pp. 31-32 and 84.
2. Gelb, op. cit., p. 36.
3. A. Ungnad, *Subartu,* Berlin, 1936; B. Hrozny, *Ancient History of Western Asia, India and Crete,* Prague (undated), pp. 110-11; E. Herzfeld, *The Persian Empire,* Wiesbaden, 1968; H. Lewy, 'Assyria c. 2600-1816 BC', *Cambridge Ancient History,* 3rd ed., Vol. 1, Part 2, pp. 730-32.
4. Gelb, op. cit.; same author, 'New Light on Hurrians and Subarians', *Studi orientalistici in onore di G. Levi della Vida,* Vol. 1 (1956), pp. 378-92.
5. B. Hrouda, 'Die Churriter als Problem archäologischer Forschungen', *Archaeologia Geographica,* Vol. 7 (1958), pp. 14-19.
6. Lewy, op. cit., pp. 730-31; Hrozny, op. cit., p. 26.
7. Gelb left this question 'for another occasion' in his *Hurrians and Subarians* (p. 84) and apparently has not seen fit to take it up since.
8. This suggestion which was first made by Ida Bobula in her *Sumerian affiliations,* Washington, 1951 and has since been adopted by other writers, is not as far-fetched as it might seem at first sight. The name of Subartu as a geographical designation survived well into the sixth century BC by which time the Armenians had become firmly established in their present homeland. It is entirely possible that at that stage, the peoples living in the neighbourhood of the Magyars were still conscious of their Subarian origin and were calling them by some such name. Thereafter, this name or a distorted form of it, Sevordik, was preserved by the Armenians and ultimately reached Constantinus. By that time, of course, the origin of the name was long forgotten.
9. Gelb, op. cit., p. 55.
10. Gelb, op. cit., p. 39.
11. W. Hinz, 'Persia c. 2400-1800 BC', *Cambridge Ancient History,* 3rd ed., Vol. 1, Part 2, p. 659.
12. C. J. Gadd, 'Babylonia c. 2120-1800 BC', *Cambridge Ancient History,* 3rd ed., Vol. 1, Part 2, p. 617.
13. A. Salonen, *Hippologia Accadica,* Helsinki, 1955, pp. 16-17.
14. Gelb, op. cit., pp. 41-42.

15. Gelb, op. cit., pp. 65-70. I have adjusted the regnal years given by Gelb in accordance with the dates stated in the revised (3rd) edition of the *Cambridge Ancient History*.
16. A. Götze, *Hethiter, Churriter und Assyrer*, Oslo, 1936, p. 106; C. Burney and D. M. Lang, *The peoples of the hills*, London, 1971, p. 49.
17. Burney and Lang, op. cit., pp. 43-49.
18. Ungnad, op. cit., pp. 131 and 136.
19. Hrozny, op. cit., p. 111.
20. Gelb makes the point that the native Hurrian term for the state of Mitanni was Hurri and that Tushratta, king of Mitanni, called himself 'the Hurrian king': Gelb, op. cit., pp. 72, 75.
21. R. de Vaux, 'Les Hurrites de l'histoire et les Horites de la bible', *Académie des inscriptions et belles lettres, Comptes rendues*, 1967, pp. 427-36.
22. J. Wiesner, 'Die Kulturen der frühen Reitervölker', *Handbuch der Kulturgeschichte*. Vol. 2, Frankfurt, 1968, p. 14.
23. E. Dayton, 'The problem of tin in the Ancient World', *World Archaeology*, Vol. 3 (1971), pp. 49-70, at p. 63.
24. Vaux, op. cit., pp. 428-29.
25. W. F. Albright and T. O. Lambdin, 'The evidence of language', *Cambridge Ancient History*, Revised edition, Fasc. 54, 1966, p. 33.
26. Gelb, op. cit., p. 68.
27. E. A. Speiser, 'The Hurrian participation in the civilisations of Mesopotamia, Syria and Palestine', *Cahiers d'histoire mondiale*, Vol. 1 (1953), pp. 311-27, at p. 312; H. G. Güterbock, 'The Hurrian element in the Hittite empire', *Cahiers d'histoire mondiale*, Vol. 2 (1954), pp. 383-94.
28. H. Lewy, op. cit., p. 733.
29. M. S. Drower, 'Ugarit', *Cambridge Ancient History*, Revised edition, 1968; p. 9; A. Kammenhuber, 'Die neuen hurrischen Texte aus Ugarit', *Ugarit-Forschungen*, Vol. 2 (1970), pp. 295-302.
30. B. Vawter, *A path through Genesis*, London, 1966; p. 100; *The Jerusalem Bible*, pp. 1408-09.
31. Seton Lloyd, *Early highland peoples of Anatolia*, London, 1967, p. 108; B. B. Piotrovskii, *Urartu*, London, 1967, p. 1.
32. Burney and Lang, op. cit., p. 167.
33. It is generally accepted that the name Gomer in Gen. 10 represents the Cimmerians: see E. D. Phillips, 'The Scythian domination in Western Asia: its record in history, scripture and archaeology', *World Archaeology*, Vol. 4 (1972), pp. 129-38, at p. 133.

34. Piotrovskii, op. cit., pp. 6-7.
35. Wiesner, op. cit., p. 35.
36. Burney and Lang, op. cit., pp. 143, 146-47.
37. Burney and Lang, op. cit., pp. 171-72; R. A. Crossland, 'Immigrants from the North', *Cambridge Ancient History*, Revised edition, Fasc. 60 (1967), p. 36.
38. Piotrovskii, op. cit., p. 70.
39. K. Lukácsy, *A magyarok öselei, hajdankori nevei és lakhelyei, eredeti örmény kutfök után*, Kolozsvár, 1870, pp. 223-24.
40. Burney and Lang, op. cit., pp. 171-80.
41. Lukácsy, op. cit., pp. 223-24.